CRIMSON DOMINATION

THE PROCESS BEHIND ALABAMA'S 15TH NATIONAL CHAMPIONSHIP

CRIMSON TIDE
BACK TO BACK
NATIONAL
CHAMPIONS
2012

TOMMY FORD & MARK MAYFIELD

FOREWORD BY ELI GOLD · AFTERWORD BY BARRETT JONES

Crimson Domination: The Process Behind Alabama's 15th National Championship

ISBN: 0794839746
Printed and assembled in the United States.

- TABLE OF CONTENTS -

A Dedication To The Late Mal Moore

(1939-2013)

Twelve days after Alabama won the 2013 BCS National Championship Game in South Florida, Mal Moore stood at a podium just outside Bryant-Denny Stadium and said he wanted Crimson Tide players "to know how much I've enjoyed watching them compete, not only this year, but in their remarkable achievement of winning three national titles in four years."

Moore was far too modest to mention his own contribution to those championships. But since his passing on March 30, 2013, Alabama players and coaches have been profuse in their praise for a man who was associated with Crimson Tide sports for almost 50 years, including the last 13-plus years as UA's athletics director.

(Above left) Mal Moore played at Alabama from 1958 through 1962. (Left) Moore was an assistant coach under Paul "Bear" Bryant at UA from 1964 to 1982, and again from 1990 to 1993 under Gene Stallings. (Opposite page, top) Moore became Alabama's associate athletics director in 1993 and moved up to athletics director in 1999. (Opposite page, bottom left) Moore looks on with Nick Saban as Terry Saban unveils a statue of the Alabama head coach. (Opposite page, bottom right) Moore acknowledges the crowd during the 2012 national championship victory parade while UA President Judy Bonner looks on.

"Nobody genuinely cared more about the Crimson Tide than Mal did," Alabama head football coach Nick Saban said of the man who hired him in 2007. "We can talk about all the championships Mal has been involved with, but I think what will be remembered most was the man he was. He always put the best interests of others ahead of his own… Mal was the No. 1 reason we decided to move to Tuscaloosa."

This book — which not only chronicles the Crimson Tide's 2012 championship season, but also the spirit of its players and coaches — is dedicated to Mal Moore.

This Team Would Not Be Denied

It was a scorching-hot day, 109 degrees in the shade, as I walked in to Cowboys Stadium in Arlington, Texas, to begin my 24th season behind the microphone as the "voice" of the Crimson Tide.

I was not surprised to feel butterflies in my ample midsection. It was, after all, the 2012 season opener. How good would this edition of the Crimson Tide be? Even though head coach Nick Saban and his staff were, in my estimation, the best in the business, let's face it, there were many NFL Draft choices and free agents who had to be replaced off of the 2011 Alabama roster, and the always scary Michigan Wolverines were the opponents. Sure, butterflies were acceptable on this steamy Texas night.

Hours later, with a 41-14 win tucked away, we made our way back to the parking lot, a wry smile on our collective faces, knowing that even though nothing ever comes easily, this team would certainly contend for a national championship — the school's 15th title.

Would back-to-back national championships be easy? Heck no. Never is. It's not supposed to be. There were injuries aplenty, terrible weather in Arkansas and even worse conditions in Missouri. A loss to the Texas A&M Aggies and a gut-wrenching, remote-control-battery-sapping night watching other title contenders lose one by one couldn't snuff out the dreams of this edition of the Tide. It seemed as though another title shot was destined to be. This hard-working, never-say-die, "we're all in this together" group of players and coaches would not be denied.

Finally, after a win over Georgia in the SEC Championship Game, only one more hurdle remained as we all headed south to Miami for the BCS National Championship Game against Notre Dame. A matchup made in football heaven, the Crimson Tide against the Fighting Irish. Jan. 7 couldn't get here fast enough for the college football fans of the nation.

We all know the result. Never doubt the Crimson Tide. That final hurdle was cleared with tons of room to spare. National championship No. 15 was heading to the trophy case in Tuscaloosa.

In this book, utilizing their "trusted insider" status, co-authors Tommy Ford and Mark Mayfield, along with photographer Kent Gidley, take you inside the special 2012 national title season. The players, the coaches, the highs, the lows and the quest to be the best are all inside this book. I think you will especially enjoy the profiles on the seniors who won three national titles in their careers at Alabama. This is their story told as only Tommy, Mark and Kent can tell it.

Enjoy the memories, and Roll Tide!

— Eli Gold,
The Voice of the Crimson Tide

THE MARCH TO NATIONAL CHAMPIONSHIP #15

GAME 1

SEPT. 1, 2012

ALABAMA
41

MICHIGAN
14

n the Crimson Tide's historic three national ch

seasons within a four-year span, each team cou

least one "statement" game each fall — a conte

nation, not to mention the Alabama faithful, took no

For the 2009 team, it was the SEC Champior

beatdown of top-ranked and defending nationa

Florida and its star quarterback, Tim Tebow.

The massive video board at Cowboys Stadium in Arlington, Texas, looks down at Alabama's M

performs prior to the Crimson Tide's neutral-site op

(Below) Running back T.J. Yeldon (4) goes for part of his 111 rushing yards in the 41-14 victory over Michigan. His 1-yard touchdown run in the fourth quarter accounted for the Tide's final points against the Wolverines. (Opposite page, inset): Dee Milliner (28) returns an interception 35 yards in the first quarter to set up Alabama's third touchdown of the period.

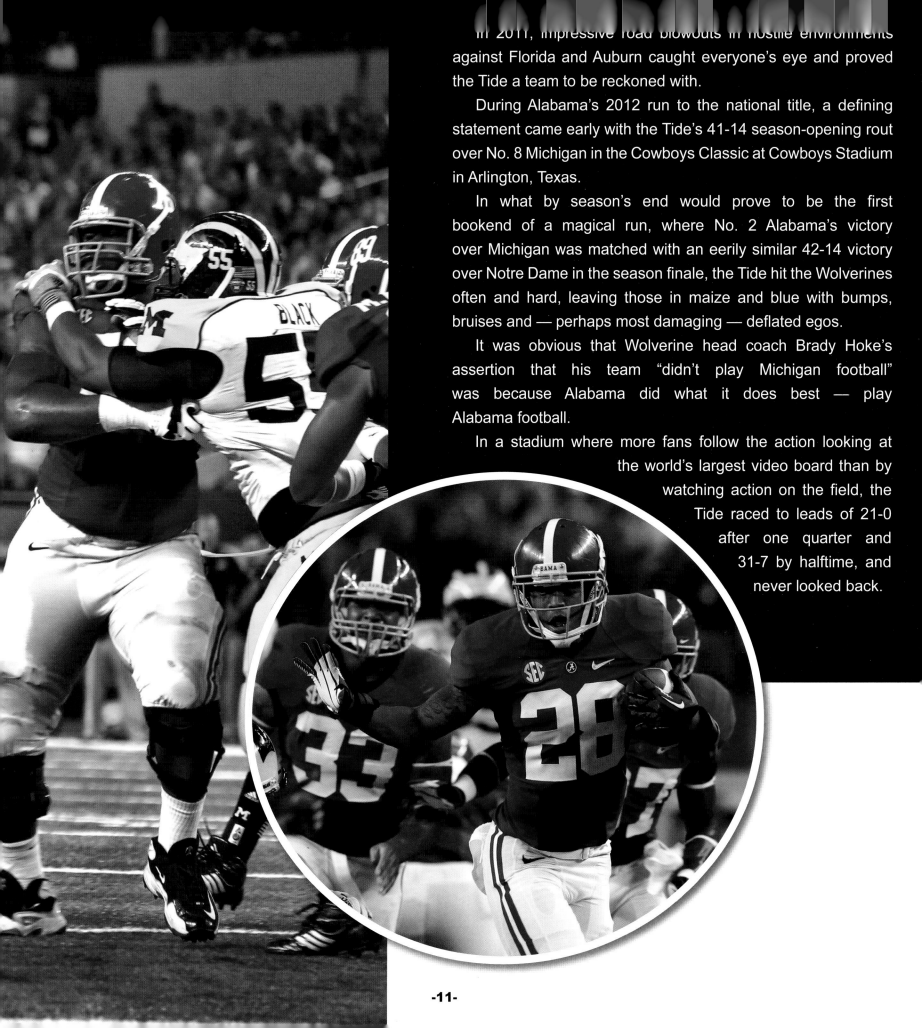

In 2011, impressive road blowouts in hostile environments against Florida and Auburn caught everyone's eye and proved the Tide a team to be reckoned with.

During Alabama's 2012 run to the national title, a defining statement came early with the Tide's 41-14 season-opening rout over No. 8 Michigan in the Cowboys Classic at Cowboys Stadium in Arlington, Texas.

In what by season's end would prove to be the first bookend of a magical run, where No. 2 Alabama's victory over Michigan was matched with an eerily similar 42-14 victory over Notre Dame in the season finale, the Tide hit the Wolverines often and hard, leaving those in maize and blue with bumps, bruises and — perhaps most damaging — deflated egos.

It was obvious that Wolverine head coach Brady Hoke's assertion that his team "didn't play Michigan football" was because Alabama did what it does best — play Alabama football.

In a stadium where more fans follow the action looking at the world's largest video board than by watching action on the field, the Tide raced to leads of 21-0 after one quarter and 31-7 by halftime, and never looked back.

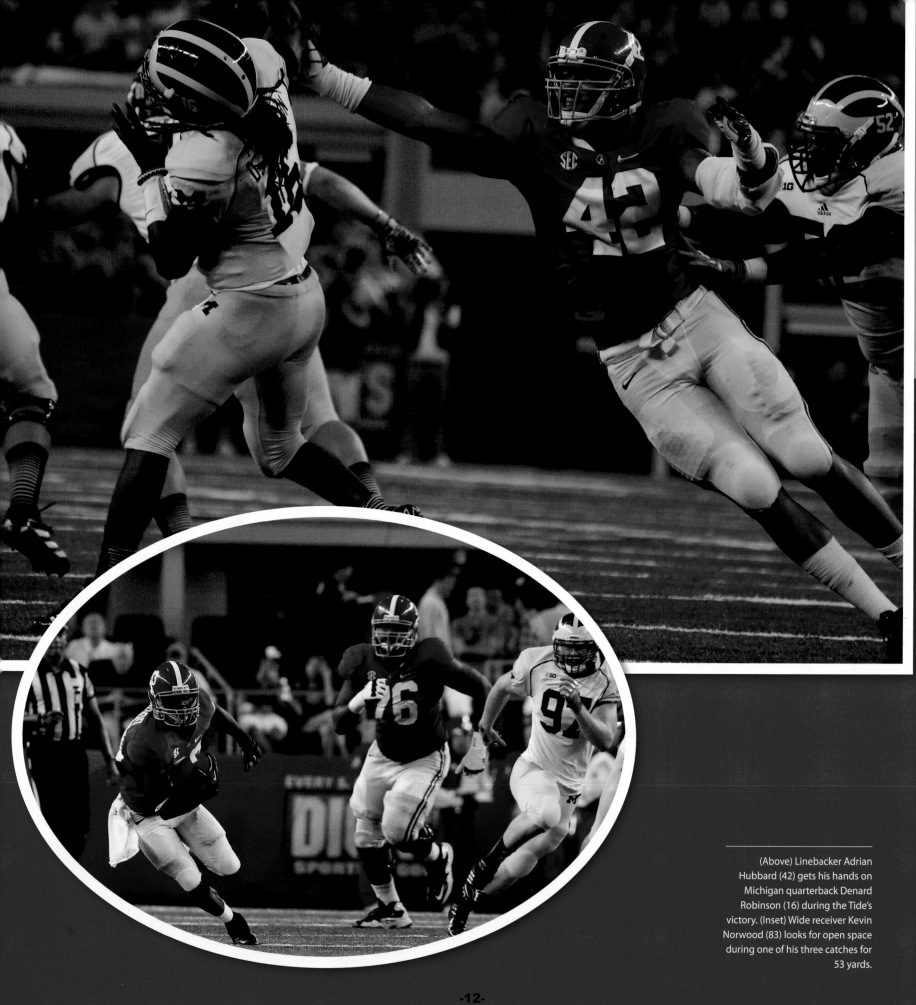

(Above) Linebacker Adrian Hubbard (42) gets his hands on Michigan quarterback Denard Robinson (16) during the Tide's victory. (Inset) Wide receiver Kevin Norwood (83) looks for open space during one of his three catches for 53 yards.

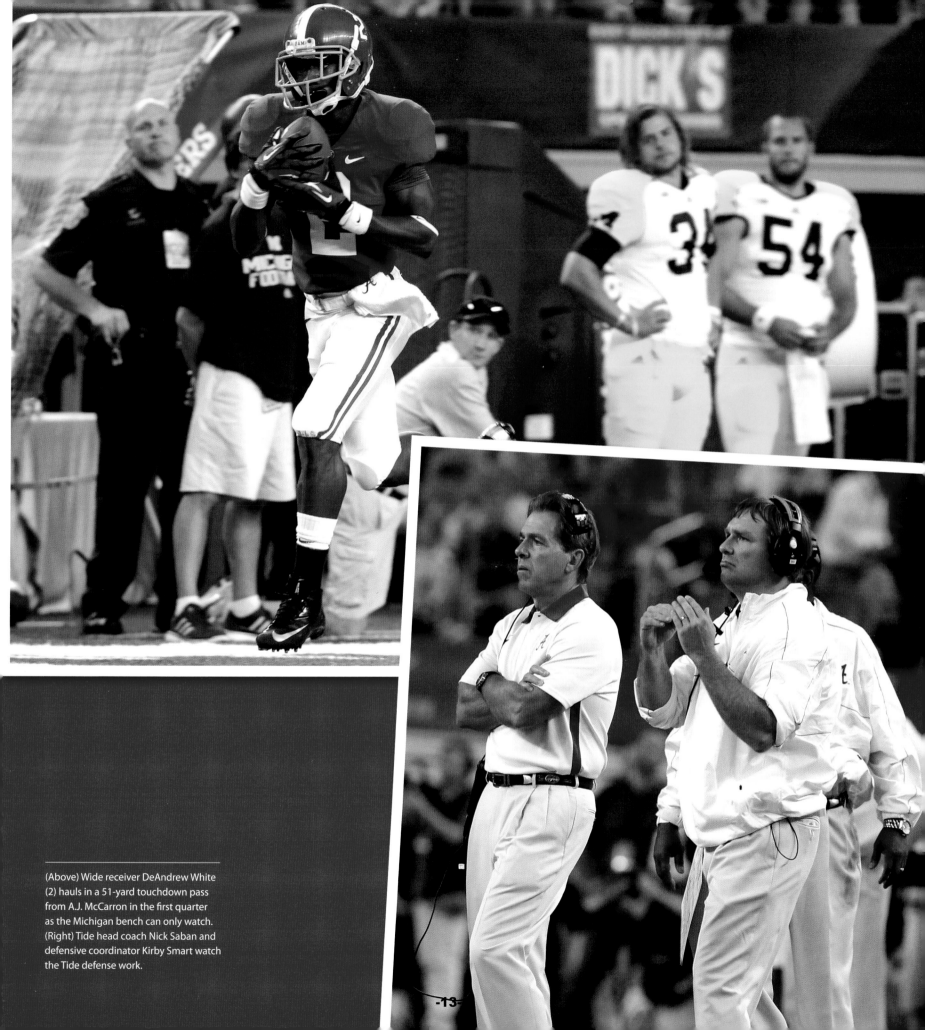

(Above) Wide receiver DeAndrew White (2) hauls in a 51-yard touchdown pass from A.J. McCarron in the first quarter as the Michigan bench can only watch. (Right) Tide head coach Nick Saban and defensive coordinator Kirby Smart watch the Tide defense work.

McCarron (10) hands off to Yeldon. McCarron completed 11 of 21 passes for 199 yards and two touchdowns in the rout of Michigan.

Picking right up from his sparkling BCS National Championship Game performance from the previous season, Tide quarterback A.J. McCarron threw to eight different receivers for 199 yards and two touchdowns against the Wolverines. A stable of Alabama running backs — led by true freshman T.J. Yeldon's record-setting 111 yards — rushed for 232 yards behind an offensive line considered the finest in college football. The performance prompted Hoke to comment, "We couldn't establish the line of scrimmage, and when you can't do that, that doesn't do you very well. It was bad on both sides of the ball."

Despite the Tide's dominance, head coach Nick Saban used the victory as a learning tool for the road ahead.

"I thought the players did a great job of competing in the game, played with a lot of energy and toughness, and were very physical," Saban said. "There are certainly a lot of things we can improve on.

"I don't think there's one player that could sit in the locker room and tell you now there's not something that we could work to improve on, and we certainly need to focus on that in the future."

Saban was prophetically correct. For this Alabama team, the best was yet to come.

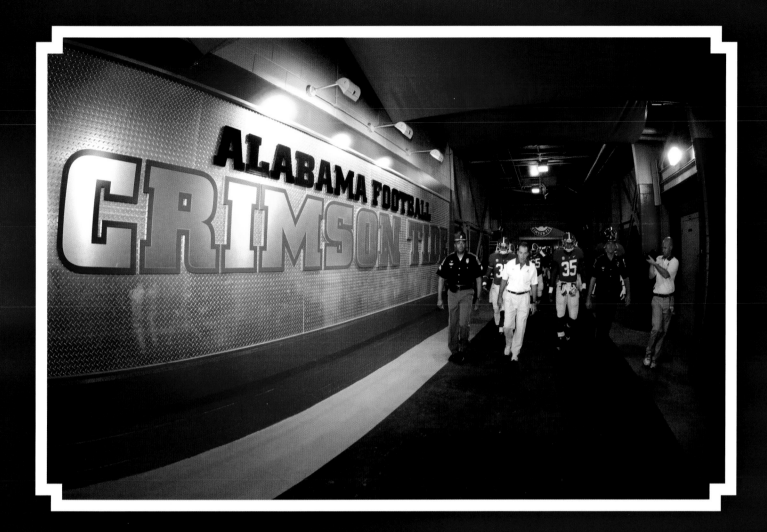

ALABAMA
35

WESTERN KENTUCKY
0

On the surface, even to this day, top-ranked Alabama's 35-0 shutout of the Western Kentucky Hilltoppers implies yet another dominating performance by the defending national champions. Scores, though, can be deceiving. Reading between the lines — or in this case, between the statistics — this game was much closer than the final margin.

Alabama head coach Nick Saban leads his team down the tunnel to Bryant-Denny Stadium before the Crimson Tide's home opener against Western Kentucky.

The Tide offensive line, highly praised for its superior performance against Michigan the previous week, met its match against the run-stop-oriented Hilltoppers, at least on this day. Contributing to Alabama's surprisingly low 103 rushing yards were six sacks of quarterback A.J. McCarron.

The Tide's defense, led by linebacker C.J. Mosley's 11 tackles, bent but didn't break, allowing Western Kentucky 224 yards, including 178 through the air.

The Tide also proved to be opportunistic, taking advantage of four Hilltopper turnovers and a four-touchdown throwing performance by McCarron. In all, the junior signal caller was 14 of 19 for 219 yards. For the first time since 1950, two receivers — Kevin Norwood and Christion Jones — caught two touchdown passes in the same game.

"There are certainly a lot of things that we need to work on and improve going into SEC play," said Saban, whose team recorded its seventh shutout during his tenure as Alabama's coach. "Arkansas is going to be a challenging game for us."

No one — not even Saban — expected what was about to transpire in Fayetteville the next week.

(Preceding page and above) Quarterback A.J. McCarron completed 14 of 19 passes for 219 yards and four touchdowns in the 35-0 victory over WKU. (Preceding page, insert) Kevin Norwood (83) catches one of his two touchdowns as part of a three-reception, 92-yard day.

(Left) Wide receiver Christion Jones catches one of his two touchdown receptions against the Hilltoppers. (Inset) Running back Kenyan Drake (17) races to a 32-yard touchdown late in the fourth quarter.

(Above) Linebackers Trey DePriest (33) and Nico Johnson (35) stop Western Kentucky fullback Kadeem Jones (32). (Right) Christion Jones (22) and DeAndrew White (2) celebrate one of Jones' two TD catches.

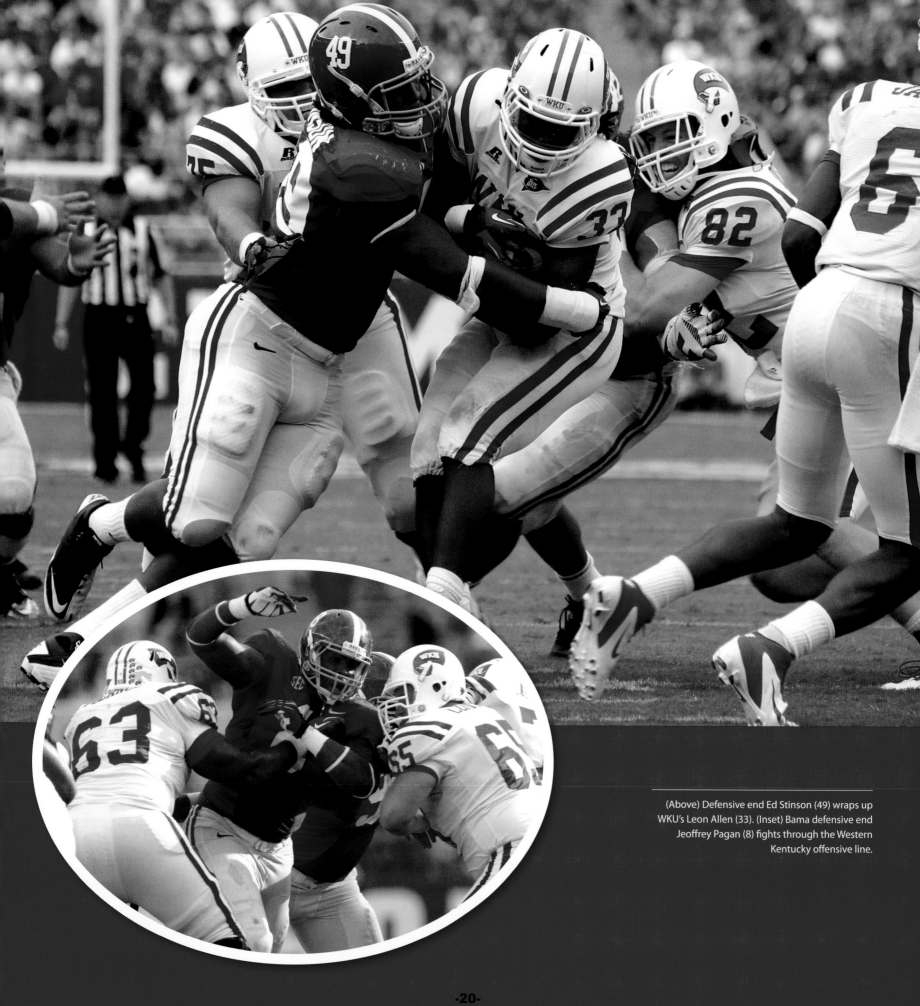

(Above) Defensive end Ed Stinson (49) wraps up WKU's Leon Allen (33). (Inset) Bama defensive end Jeoffrey Pagan (8) fights through the Western Kentucky offensive line.

ALABAMA
52

ARKANSAS
0

pon preseason examination of the Cri____ 2012 football schedule, Alabama fans f____ circled three games — Michigan in neut____ Texas, along with road games at Arkansas a____ as potential stumbling blocks to repeating____ national champions.

Eddie Lacy (42) splits the Arkansas defense for one of his three touchdown runs in the victo____

(Above) Christion Jones (22) makes one of his three receptions for 74 yards in the shutout of Arkansas as the Hogs' Rohan Gaines (26) tries to bring him down. (Inset) Reserve quarterback Blake Sims (6) dives in to cap off a 27-yard fourth-quarter touchdown run in the rainy conditions in Fayetteville.

Three weeks into the season, only one circle remained. On a rainy and blustery day in Fayetteville, the Tide dismantled a dysfunctional Arkansas team 52-0 in the most lopsided victory of the 21-game series. In SEC games, it was Alabama's largest margin of victory since defeating Auburn 55-0 in 1948. For the Razorbacks, it was their first shutout in almost a half-century.

Tide running back Eddie Lacy powered through the Arkansas defense for three touchdowns, the Alabama defense forced five turnovers and the A.J. McCarron-led offense rolled to 438 total yards.

(Inset) Head coach Nick Saban and his assistants watched Alabama's largest margin of victory in an SEC game since a 1948 beating of rival Auburn. (Above) Safety Vinnie Sunseri (3) intercepts a pass by Arkansas' Brandon Allen in the second quarter.

(Left) T.J. Yeldon (4) rushes for part of his 57-yard, one-touchdown day against the Razorbacks. (Below) Tight end Michael Williams (89) pulls away from the Arkansas defense after one of his two receptions.

Defensive end Quinton Dial (90) looks down at the Arkansas quarterback after a tackle.

For the Hogs, the Tide's final margin was salt in the wound to an already-bizarre year. First, it was an offseason scandal that cost head coach Bobby Petrino his job. Then, the week before the Alabama game, Arkansas was upset by Louisiana-Monroe and lost star quarterback Tyler Wilson to injury, and he did not play against the Tide.

Following the game, a visibly upset Wilson challenged his Razorback teammates. "Do I feel that we, at times, gave up out there? Absolutely. As a leader, it sucks to see people not do their jobs and to see things go wrong."

At the end of the season, Arkansas did not retain "interim" head coach John L. Smith and hired Bret Bielema away from Big Ten Conference champion Wisconsin.

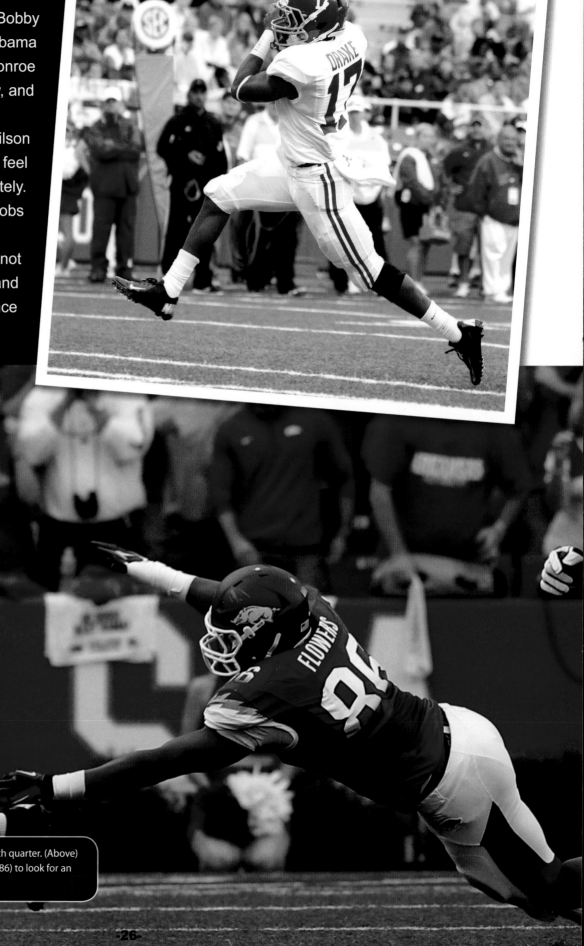

(Top) Kenyan Drake (17) runs for a 12-yard touchdown early in the fourth quarter. (Above) Quarterback A.J. McCarron (10) slips away from Arkansas' Trey Flowers (86) to look for an open receiver in the shutout victory over the Hogs.

ALABAMA
40

FLORIDA ATLANTIC
7

As ugly as the Crimson Tide's first two plays were against the Florida Atlantic Owls, the third play made up for them, and more.

From Alabama's 15-yard line:

- Play 1: A.J. McCarron pass complete to Michael Williams for a loss of 3 yards;
- No play: False start on Alabama, 5-yard penalty;
- Play 2: Eddie Lacy rushes for 8 yards;
- Play 3: A.J. McCarron passes to Kenny Bell on a crossing pattern for 85 yards and a touchdown.

The Alabama cheerleaders and Big Al lead the cheers before the Tide's home game against Florida Atlantic.

(Above and opposite page) Backup quarterback Blake Sims (6) hands off to Kenyan Drake (17). Drake rushed for a touchdown in the victory over the Owls. (Opposite page, inset) Cyrus Jones (8) shakes off a FAU defender during his 35-yard reception.

(Left) Jesse Williams (54) leaps to block a pass by FAU quarterback Graham Wilbert. (Below) Williams blocks a 48-yard field-goal attempt by FAU kicker Vinny Zaccario (39) in the first quarter.

-30-

In tennis terms, in only a few seconds, it was "Game, set, match."

Before most of the Alabama fans could scream a good "Roll Tide," the Tide led 7-0, and the rout was on. Alabama put points on the board on six consecutive first-half possessions, roaring to a 30-0 halftime lead and coasting to a 40-7 win. Lacy paced the Tide running game with 106 yards on 15 carries. McCarron finished 15 of 25 for 212 yards and three touchdowns.

With the game's outcome settled early, the only question was whether the Alabama defense, despite playing backups most of the way, could get its third straight shutout — a feat not accomplished since 1966. With just under three minutes left in the game, though, the Owls scored on a short touchdown toss.

"We pride ourselves on teams not scoring on our defense," said Tide defensive back Dee Milliner. "That's a big accomplishment for us. But even though they got in, we still had a great game."

(Above) Sims (6) rushes through the FAU defense during the fourth quarter. He had six carries as Alabama was able to play several reserves in the second half.
(Left) Robert Lester (37) keeps his eyes on the Florida Atlantic offense.

Cyrus Kouandjio (71) moves into pass protection as FAU's David Baptiste (93) begins his rush toward the quarterback.

ALABAMA
33

OLE MISS
14

For 10 games of regulation football — sin[ ] contest with Tennessee — Alabama had ne[ ]

On a spectacular fall evening in sold[ ] Denny Stadium, where the Tide's 1992 national[ ] were honored in pregame ceremonies, a determin[ ] squad would change that — for all of 15 seconds.

The Alabama student section brings the noise during the Alabama-Ole Miss game in [ ]

Jeremy Shelley field goals (each from 38 yards), the Rebels methodically drove 75 yards in 13 plays to take a 7-6 lead. On the subsequent kickoff, the Tide's Christion Jones scampered down the home sideline for a 99-yard touchdown return, giving Alabama a lead that it would never relinquish.

Following Jones' heroics, over the next four minutes Tide defensive backs Dee Milliner, Robert Lester and Deion Belue each picked off Ole Miss passes, leading to two touchdown tosses from A.J. McCarron to freshman sensation Amari Cooper. In the process, McCarron broke Brodie Croyle's mark for consecutive pass attempts without an interception.

(Opposite page, bottom) Amari Cooper (9) grabs a touchdown pass over the outstretched arms of Ole Miss defensive back Frank Crawford. Cooper caught a pair of TD passes in the victory over the Rebels. (Above) Christion Jones (22) races down the field during his 99-yard kickoff return for a second-quarter touchdown that gave the Tide the lead for good.

A.J. McCarron drops back to pass as center Barrett Jones scans the Ole Miss defensive line.

(Top) Robert Lester (37) returns an interception 20 yards in the second quarter as Rebels offensive lineman Pierce Burton (71) gives chase. (Inset) Eddie Lacy (42) breaks a tackle for some of his 82 rushing yards against Ole Miss.

The Alabama defense, led by linebackers C.J. Mosley (32) and Adrian Hubbard (42), bottle up a Rebels ballcarrier during the Tide's victory over Ole Miss.

Despite their 27-7 halftime deficit, the Rebels would continue to battle, scoring the second half's only touchdown. Two fourth-quarter Shelley field goals secured Alabama's 33-14 victory.

"You have to give Ole Miss a lot of credit," said head coach Nick Saban. "They played hard with a lot of toughness. We had a lot of respect for their team coming in, but nobody really listens to me until after the fact, and they say, 'Yeah, you were right.'"

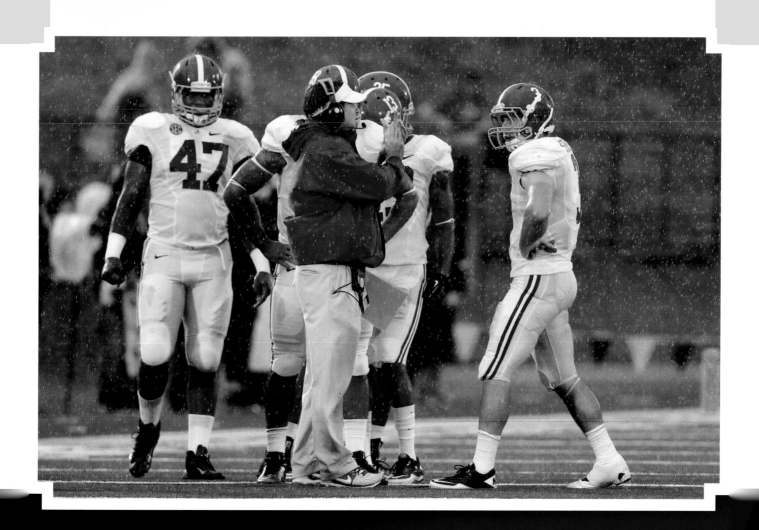

ALABAMA
42

MISSOURI
10

W hen the day was done, forecasters ir
Missouri area had been exactly right
of historical proportions had indeed ro
the area.

And, the weather was lousy, too.

The first storm surge came from the top-ranked C
as running backs Eddie Lacy (177 yards, three touch
T.J. Yeldon (144 yards, two touchdowns) led an
new SEC foe Missouri. Despite deplorable playing

The Crimson Tide had to deal with the elements at Missouri, as strong storms battered the te
in Columbia, and Alaba

Eddie Lacy (42) sticks the football over the pile for a touchdown. Lacy rushed for three TDs in the 42-10 victory over Missouri.

Alabama quarterback A.J. McCarron completed 16 of 21 passes for 171 yards. In total, the Tide offense racked up 533 yards, while the Alabama defenders limited the spread-happy Tigers to 129 yards and one field goal.

The second storm surge came from Mother Nature. Days out, forecasters had predicted severe weather for the Columbia area, and they didn't disappoint. Cold wind and rain battered the players and fans throughout the game.

(Below) A Missouri defender tries to bring down T.J. Yeldon. Yeldon rushed for 144 yards and two touchdowns to help pace the Tide attack.

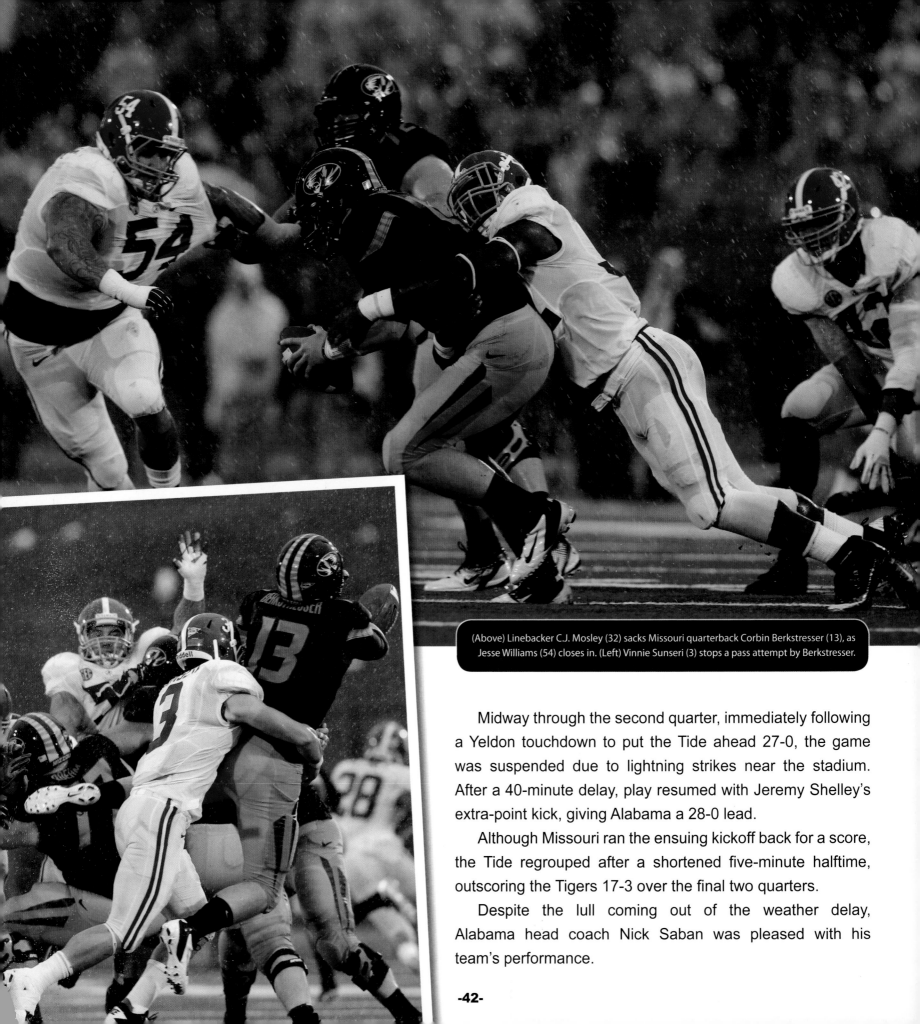

(Above) Linebacker C.J. Mosley (32) sacks Missouri quarterback Corbin Berkstresser (13), as Jesse Williams (54) closes in. (Left) Vinnie Sunseri (3) stops a pass attempt by Berkstresser.

Midway through the second quarter, immediately following a Yeldon touchdown to put the Tide ahead 27-0, the game was suspended due to lightning strikes near the stadium. After a 40-minute delay, play resumed with Jeremy Shelley's extra-point kick, giving Alabama a 28-0 lead.

Although Missouri ran the ensuing kickoff back for a score, the Tide regrouped after a shortened five-minute halftime, outscoring the Tigers 17-3 over the final two quarters.

Despite the lull coming out of the weather delay, Alabama head coach Nick Saban was pleased with his team's performance.

Nico Johnson (35) flies in to tackle a Missouri runner. Johnson had two tackles in the victory over the Tigers.

"Our players really managed things right under difficult circumstances — playing on the road in a new place in the SEC and especially with the weather conditions," Saban said. "I was really pleased with the energy, intensity and focus that we came out and started the game with.

"It's pretty obvious that when we have a high level of focus and attention to detail, we execute well and we play well."

With half the season still to play, Saban's statement would ring so true.

(Right) Wide receiver Kenny Bell (7) hauls in a pass against the Tigers. Bell had a pair of receptions for 46 yards. (Below) Wide receiver Cyrus Jones (8) fends off Missouri's Will Ebner (32) for a short gain.

GAME 7

ALABAMA
44

TENNESSEE
13

For Crimson Tide fans who love the Alabama-Tennessee rivalry, especially on the traditional "Third Saturday in October" and when it's played in Knoxville's Neyland Stadium — with the Tennessee River and the Smoky Mountains as the panoramic majestic backdrop — the 2012 game was absolute heaven.

Head coach Nick Saban and the Crimson Tide wait to take the field at Neyland Stadium against Tennessee.

(Above) Wide receiver Amari Cooper (9) makes a catch in front of Tennessee's Prentiss Waggner (23). Cooper had seven receptions for 162 yards and two touchdowns against the Vols. (Inset) T.J. Yeldon rushes for part of his 129 yards against Tennessee. Yeldon scored twice in the 44-13 victory.

The final 44-13 score was indicative of just how fun this game was for Alabama, especially on offense. Stars were plenty, but none shone brighter than true freshman Amari Cooper, whose 162 receiving yards was the most ever by an Alabama freshman in a single game. Cooper's performance earned him SEC Freshman of the Week honors and marked the fourth straight time the Tide had a 100-yard receiver in each of its last four trips to Knoxville — Julio Jones in 2010, Jones in 2008 and D.J. Hall in 2006.

Tossing those passes to Cooper was quarterback A.J. McCarron, who finished with a career-high 306 yards passing and four touchdowns, two of which were to Cooper. Freshman T.J. Yeldon's 129-yard outing highlighted Alabama's 233-yard rushing effort.

On the defensive side, the Tide — paced by C.J. Mosley, Xzavier Dickson, Damion Square, Vinnie Sunseri and Trey DePriest — held the Vols to 282 yards, including only 79 on the ground.

Eddie Lacy eludes a pair of Tennessee defenders for a big gain. Lacy rushed for 79 yards on 17 carries.

(Above, and opposite page) Kenny Bell (7) protects the football from Tennessee's Byron Moore (3) during Bell's 39-yard touchdown reception in the fourth quarter, as Christion Jones (22) tries to run interference. Bell had two catches for 68 yards.

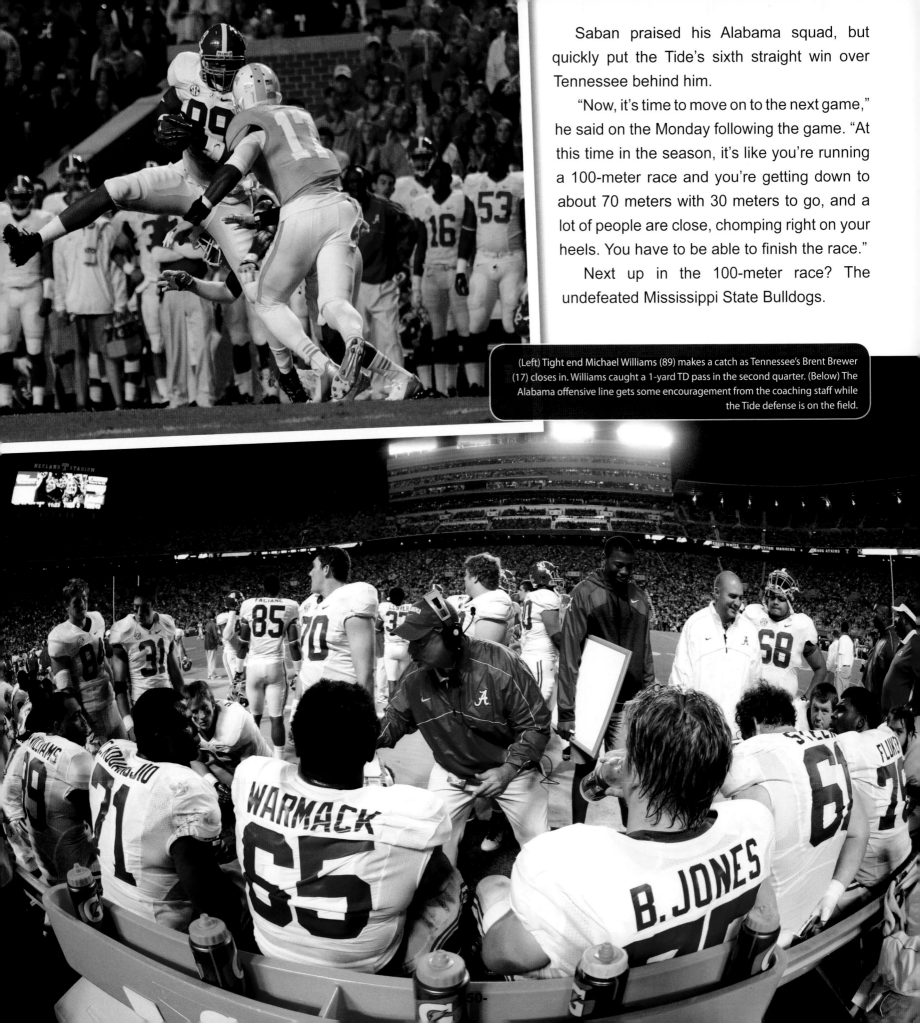

Saban praised his Alabama squad, but quickly put the Tide's sixth straight win over Tennessee behind him.

"Now, it's time to move on to the next game," he said on the Monday following the game. "At this time in the season, it's like you're running a 100-meter race and you're getting down to about 70 meters with 30 meters to go, and a lot of people are close, chomping right on your heels. You have to be able to finish the race."

Next up in the 100-meter race? The undefeated Mississippi State Bulldogs.

(Left) Tight end Michael Williams (89) makes a catch as Tennessee's Brent Brewer (17) closes in. Williams caught a 1-yard TD pass in the second quarter. (Below) The Alabama offensive line gets some encouragement from the coaching staff while the Tide defense is on the field.

ALABAMA
38

MISSISSIPPI STATE
7

or the entire week leading up to the Alabama-Mississippi State game, fans of the undefeated Bulldogs believed.

They believed so much that "This is Our State" t-shirts listing State's wins over Alabama schools Auburn, Troy and South Alabama — with the Tide next — flew off the shelves.

Lissa Handley Tyson, the great-granddaughter of legendary Tide coach Paul "Bear" Bryant, is crowned Alabama's homecoming queen during halftime festivities at the Mississippi State game.

They believed so much that on the night before the game, a t-shirt on which was crudely written "WE BELIEVE 8-0 HAIL STATE" was placed on the Paul "Bear" Bryant statue at Bryant-Denny Stadium. Within minutes, photos of the sight — and the culprit — raced into social media.

Following Alabama's 38-7 trouncing of the Bulldogs, State fans still believed. In the Crimson Tide, that is.

In very workman-like fashion, Alabama wasted no time in taking control, continuing a season trend of scoring early and often. The Tide's first three possessions resulted in three touchdowns, the first an 11-yard run by T.J. Yeldon, then touchdown tosses by A.J. McCarron to Kenny Bell (57 yards) and tight end Michael Williams (9 yards).

(Preceding page, inset) Michael Williams (89) hangs on to one of his five catches against the Bulldogs, including a 9-yard touchdown reception. (Above) T.J. Yeldon stiff-arms Mississippi State's Corey Broomfield (25) during a carry. Yeldon had 84 yards rushing, including a 11-yard TD run in the first quarter.

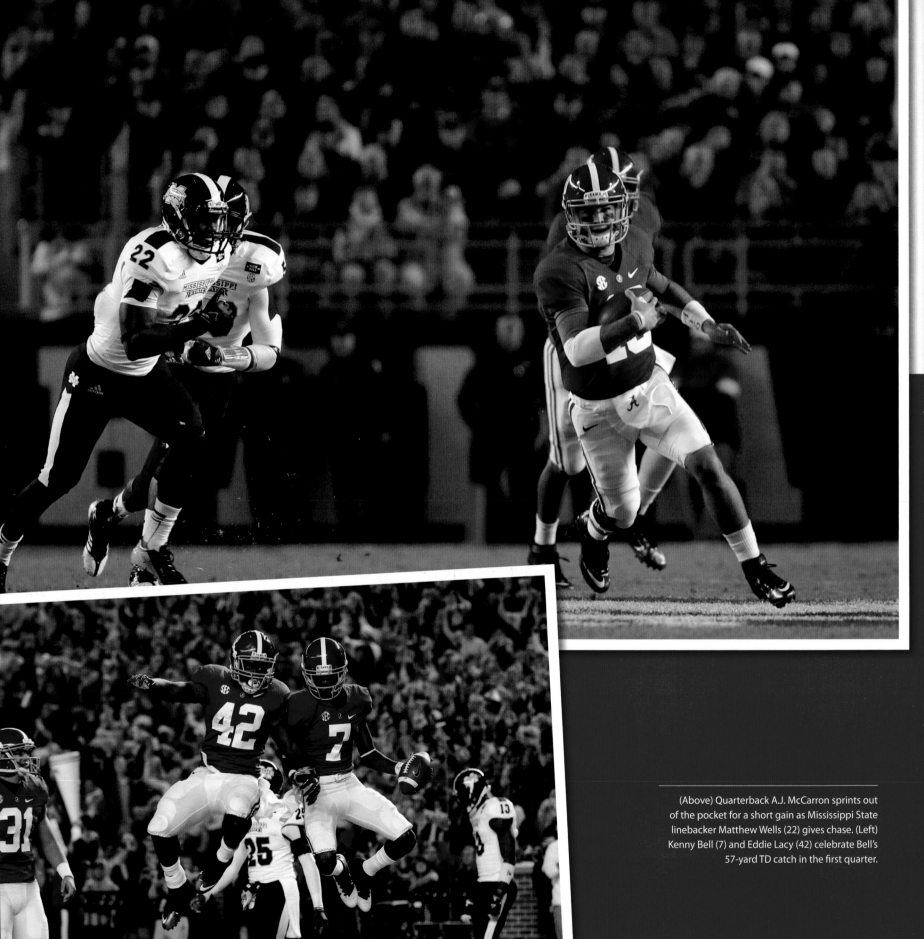

(Above) Quarterback A.J. McCarron sprints out of the pocket for a short gain as Mississippi State linebacker Matthew Wells (22) gives chase. (Left) Kenny Bell (7) and Eddie Lacy (42) celebrate Bell's 57-yard TD catch in the first quarter.

Alabama's 24-0 halftime lead ballooned to 38-0 before State scored a late touchdown against the Tide reserves.

As efficient as the offense was, the Alabama defenders were just as impressive, causing three turnovers and holding the Bulldogs to 256 yards. Defensive back Robert Lester (one interception and one fumble recovery), Vinnie Sunseri (eight tackles) and C.J. Mosley (seven tackles) paced the Tide defense.

The previous week, head coach Nick Saban used a track analogy in discussing his team's season journey. After the win over Mississippi State, boxing took the forefront.

"We certainly had a lot of respect for Mississippi State," Saban said. "You don't get to be 7-0 by accident. It was important for us to get off to a fast start in this game. You're preparing yourself to fight a 15-round fight and knowing that you're going to have to take the fight to them in the early rounds. You can't necessarily win the fight in the first round, but you can certainly lose it."

(Above) Dee Milliner (28) dives to block a 31-yard field-goal attempt by MSU's Devon Bell (40) in the first quarter.

Linebacker Adrian Hubbard (42) gets his hand on the football while it rests in the grip of Bulldog quarterback Tyler Russell (17). Hubbard had a pair of QB hurries in the game.

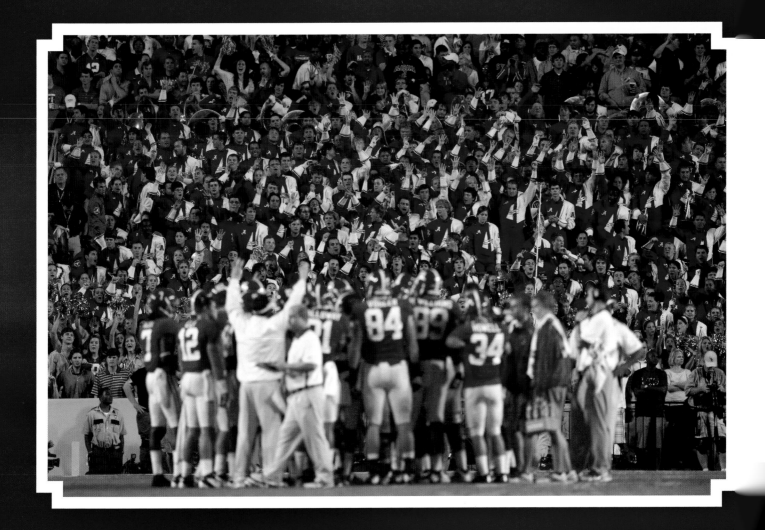

ALABAMA
21

LSU
17

I n less than six seconds — the time it took f
freshman running back T.J. Yeldon to take an A.
screen pass and race untouched for the ga
score over LSU — Death Valley became Dead Val
the 7,000-plus Tide fans, after Alabama's go-ahea
creature was left stirring in Tiger Stadium.

In front of a hostile crowd at LSU's Tiger Stadium, Alabama's Million Dollar Band lends its v

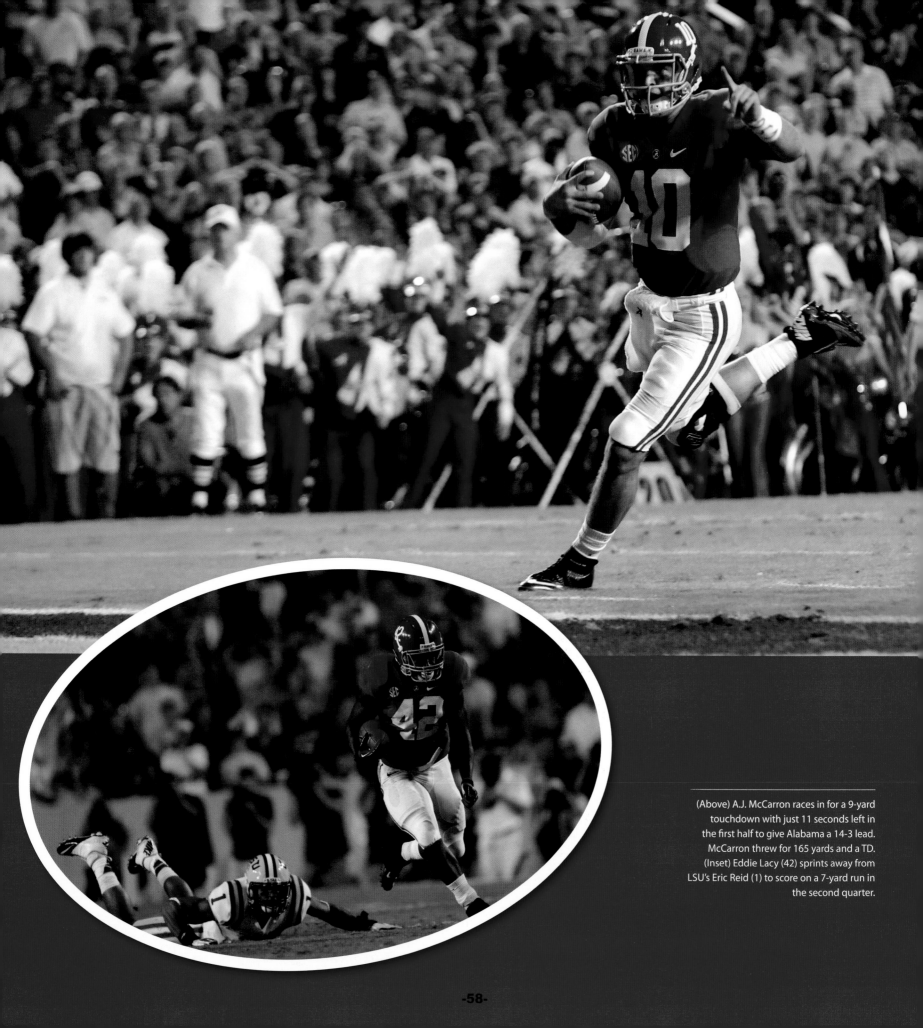

(Above) A.J. McCarron races in for a 9-yard touchdown with just 11 seconds left in the first half to give Alabama a 14-3 lead. McCarron threw for 165 yards and a TD. (Inset) Eddie Lacy (42) sprints away from LSU's Eric Reid (1) to score on a 7-yard run in the second quarter.

T.J. Yeldon eludes LSU's Barkevious Mingo (49) after catching a pass from McCarron for a 28-yard TD with 51 seconds remaining to give Alabama a 21-17 victory over the Tigers.

(Above) Kevin Norwood (83) works to get away from LSU's Jalen Collins (32). Norwood led all Alabama receivers with five catches for 62 yards. (Opposite page) Tight end Kelly Johnson (31) leaps over LSU's Ronald Martin (26) for a 10-yard reception.

Yeldon's touchdown capped a furious five-play, 72-yard drive that took all of 49 seconds.

After a dominating first half, the Tide had taken a 14-3 lead into halftime. The Tigers, behind the pinpoint passing of quarterback Zach Mettenberger, roared back to take a 17-14 lead early in the fourth quarter.

From that point to the start of Alabama's victory march, each team had two possessions. After a three-and-out series for the Tide, LSU running back Spencer Ware, on a fourth-and-1 from the Alabama 24, was stopped for no gain by D.J. Pettway and Adrian Hubbard, turning the ball over to the Tide on downs.

After another three-and-out possession by Alabama, the Tigers' next drive ended with a missed 45-yard field-goal attempt by Drew Alleman, the kicker most famous for his game-winning overtime field goal over the Tide in the 2011 "Game of the Century." Alleman's miss gave Alabama a second chance.

Taking over with 1:34 remaining at the LSU 28 and with no timeouts, the Tide's heroics commenced.

Stars were aplenty for Alabama on the final drive, but two in particular — McCarron and receiver Kevin Norwood — reached elite status. On the first play, McCarron — who had been only 1 for 7 for 0 yards in the second half — found Norwood for 18 yards over the right middle. On the next play, it was McCarron to Norwood for 15 more down the right sideline. The pair hooked up for yet another completion, this one a diving sideline catch for 11 yards to the LSU 28. Finally, much to the Tigers' relief, the McCarron-to-Norwood connection finally came to a halt with an incompletion in the back of the end zone.

(Above) Christion Jones (22) looks for extra yardage as Martin grabs hold of his jersey. Jones had four catches for 40 yards.

On second down, the cool McCarron — facing a rabid crowd, one of the best defenses in the nation and a team determined to make amends for the previous season's embarrassing national championship game loss — became legendary in Crimson Tide football lore.

Thanks to a suggestion from center Barrett Jones during an earlier timeout, the Alabama offensive staff dialed up the perfect play. As LSU came on an all-out blitz, McCarron lofted a screen pass into the hands of the freshman Yeldon, who scampered 28 yards for the game-winning score. On the Tigers' ensuing series, the Tide's Damion Square sacked Mettenberger to end the game.

In a crowded press room following the game, Saban, who called the last drive "something I'll never forget," lavished praise on his Alabama squad.

"We told our players that they would have to overcome a lot of adversity to win a game here. And when things went bad and the momentum of the game changed, that's what we kept talking to them about. And they kept their poise, and they kept playing, and they kept competing. I've never been prouder of a bunch of guys to overcome adversity."

Little did Saban know, but even greater adversity would come the next week.

The Crimson Tide takes the field with a raucous Bryant-Denny Stadium crowd behind th

GAME 10
NOV. 10, 2012

TEXAS A&M
29

ALABAMA
24

During his Heisman Trophy acceptance spe Manziel, Texas A&M's all-everything thanked the usuals for his award — the He his parents and family; his school, coaches and (especially his offensive linemen); and his high sch

He never, though, thanked the Crimson Tide, should have.

(Above) Texas A&M quarterback Johnny Manziel (2) is greeted by Damion Square (92) and Jesse Williams. (Opposite page, inset) Manziel tries to run away from the Tide's Ed Stinson (49).

Not a knock on the Tide, but without Manziel's heroics in leading his Aggies to an upset on a national stage against top-ranked Alabama, chances are good that the Heisman would have gone to runner-up Manti Te'o, Notre Dame's All-American linebacker and the most decorated defensive player in college football history.

Whether the Tide's loss could be attributed to the emotional win over LSU a week earlier is debatable, although Saban did say following the game that his team's mental energy and intensity seemed to decline as the week went on.

No matter Alabama's emotion, or lack of, one thing became perfectly clear — Manziel, a.k.a. "Johnny Football" — could indeed play some football. The redshirt freshman led his A&M team to three first-quarter scores and a 20-0 lead. In the opening quarter alone, he rushed for 74 yards and threw for another 76.

By the time the Tide defense adjusted to the fast-paced Aggie offense in the second quarter, the damage appeared to be done. Nevertheless, Alabama responded with two second-quarter touchdowns, cutting the deficit by halftime to 20-14.

(Left) Eddie Lacy (42) fights for the goal line, and finds it on a 2-yard touchdown run with 19 seconds left in the second quarter. (Below) Manziel is bottled up by Alabama defenders Quinton Dial (90) and Trey DePriest (33).

Kenny Bell (7) keeps a tight hold on the football during one of his three catches for 73 yards against the Aggies.

(Above) All the Texas A&M bench can do is watch as Amari Cooper (9) catches a 54-yard TD pass from A.J. McCarron with 6:09 left in the fourth quarter to pull the Tide to 29-24, but Alabama could not overcome the Aggies. (Inset) C.J. Mosley (32) tackles Texas A&M wide receiver Malcome Kennedy (84).

In the second half, each time the Tide inched closer, Manziel and A&M stayed just enough ahead. As challenged as Alabama was throughout the contest, though, chances were aplenty late in the game.

With 4:27 remaining, A.J. McCarron's 54-yard pass to Kenny Bell put the Tide in business at the Aggie 6-yard line. McCarron dropped back to pass but was forced to run the ball for no gain. Next, Eddie Lacy got just 1 yard around left end. McCarron took the ball to the A&M 2 on the next play. On fourth-and-goal from the 2, McCarron's pass to the right side of the end zone was intercepted.

Manziel's performance — 92 yards rushing and 24 completions in 31 passes for 253 yards and two touchdowns — was definitely Heisman-worthy, but that didn't make the Alabama players feel any better.

"We're disappointed, obviously," Tide center Barrett Jones said. "You know, just so many missed opportunities. But, you've got to give them a lot of credit. They came out with a great game plan."

Said Alabama coach Nick Saban, "We played better as the game went on, but we still didn't make the plays that we needed to make."

Nevertheless, Saban noted that his Tide team still controlled its own destiny in the SEC, and he reminded reporters that two of the three national championship teams he had coached had one loss.

"There's still a lot for this team to play for," Saban said.

ALABAMA
49

WESTERN
CAROLINA
0

n college football, it may not be possible to ge
in one day, but for the No. 3-ranked Alabama C
it happened.

The first was in mid-afternoon in Bryant-Den
where the Tide easily defeated the outmanned West
Catamounts 49-0.

Crimson Tide fans cheer on the Alabama football team as it enters the stadium during the prega
at

Head coach Nick Saban leads the Crimson Tide onto the field at Bryant-Denny Stadium. (Opposite page, inset) A.J. McCarron (10) calls the signals as the Tide offensive line, led by center Barrett Jones (75), readies for action against Western Carolina.

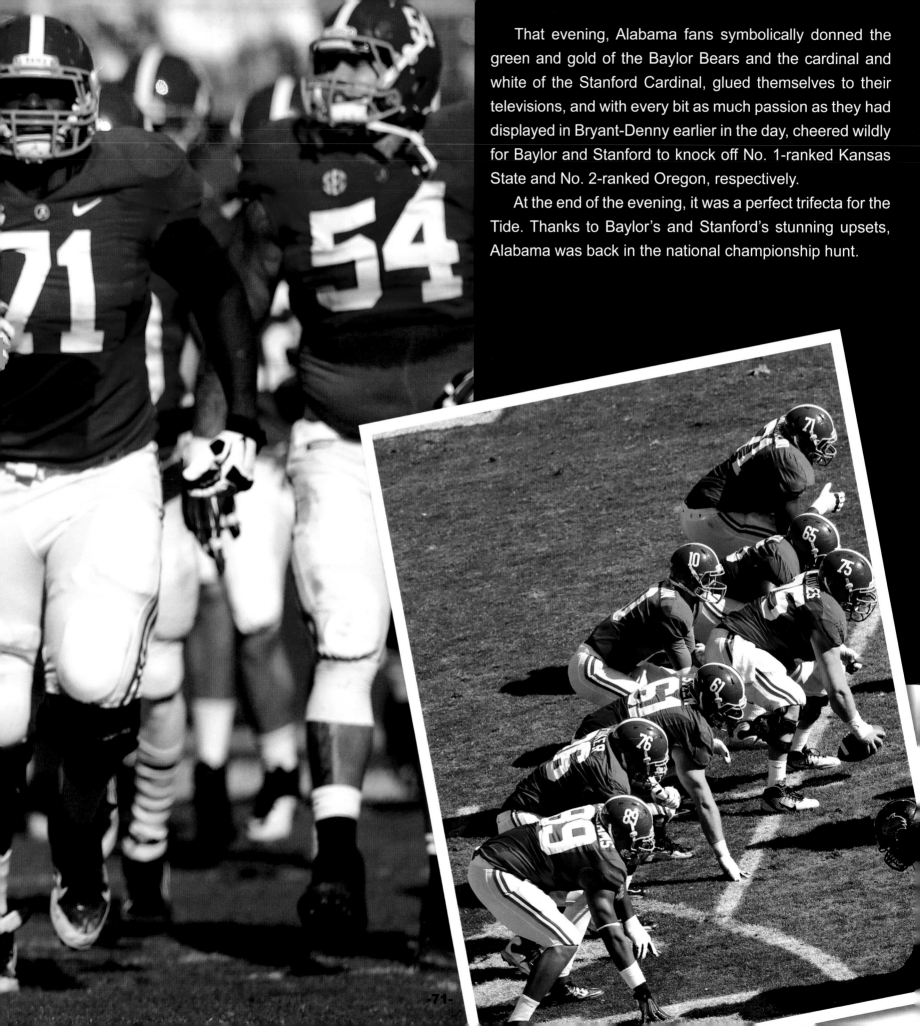

That evening, Alabama fans symbolically donned the green and gold of the Baylor Bears and the cardinal and white of the Stanford Cardinal, glued themselves to their televisions, and with every bit as much passion as they had displayed in Bryant-Denny earlier in the day, cheered wildly for Baylor and Stanford to knock off No. 1-ranked Kansas State and No. 2-ranked Oregon, respectively.

At the end of the evening, it was a perfect trifecta for the Tide. Thanks to Baylor's and Stanford's stunning upsets, Alabama was back in the national championship hunt.

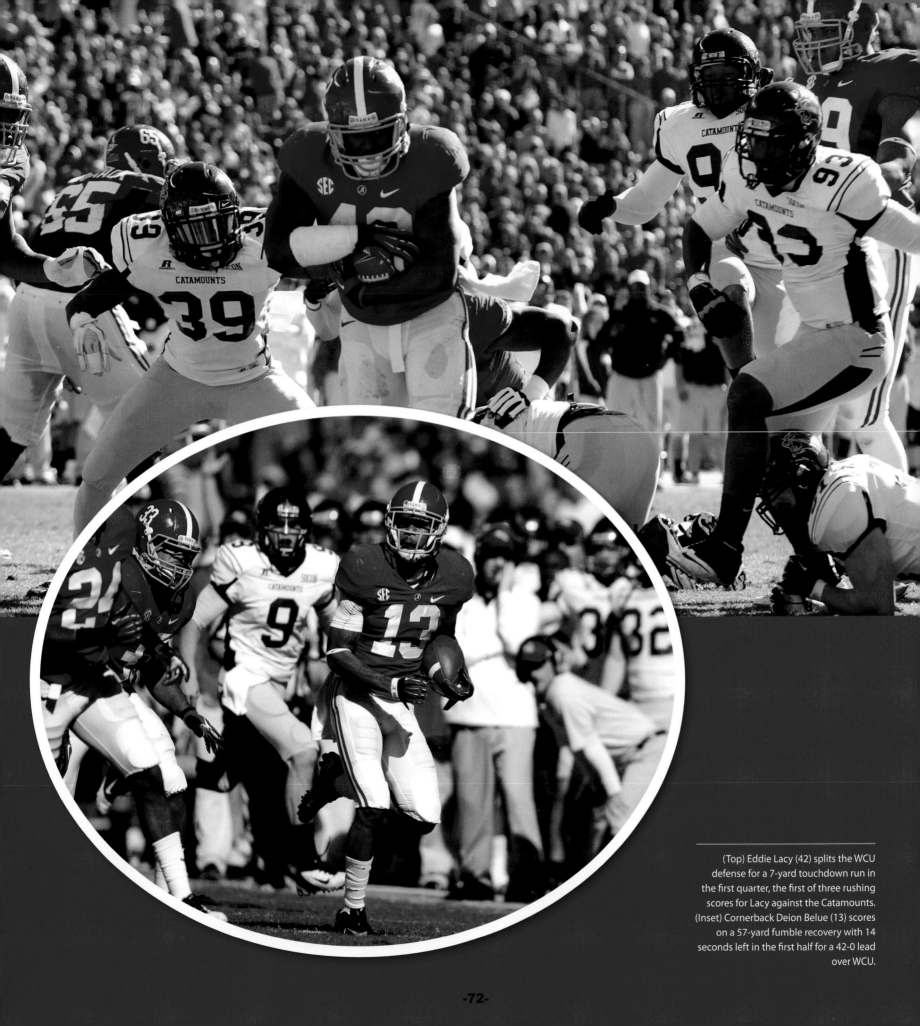

(Top) Eddie Lacy (42) splits the WCU defense for a 7-yard touchdown run in the first quarter, the first of three rushing scores for Lacy against the Catamounts. (Inset) Cornerback Deion Belue (13) scores on a 57-yard fumble recovery with 14 seconds left in the first half for a 42-0 lead over WCU.

Against the Catamounts, Tide running back Eddie Lacy scored three first-half touchdowns, T.J. Yeldon added another and A.J. McCarron broke an Alabama single-season record with his 21st touchdown pass — a 29-yard strike to Christion Jones. The Tide jumped out to a 42-0 first-half lead, emptied the bench for the second half and coasted to the easy win.

Despite the euphoria over Alabama once again controlling its own destiny, head coach Nick Saban dismissed all talk of it at his Monday news conference.

"We're trying to work our way into a conversation by how we play," Saban said. "We're not trying to hold a position (in the BCS). We're trying to create one by how we play."

"Everybody in this organization needs to understand that we're dismissing all talk about anything except playing Auburn," Saban continued. "The Iron Bowl is a big deal. It's a legendary game."

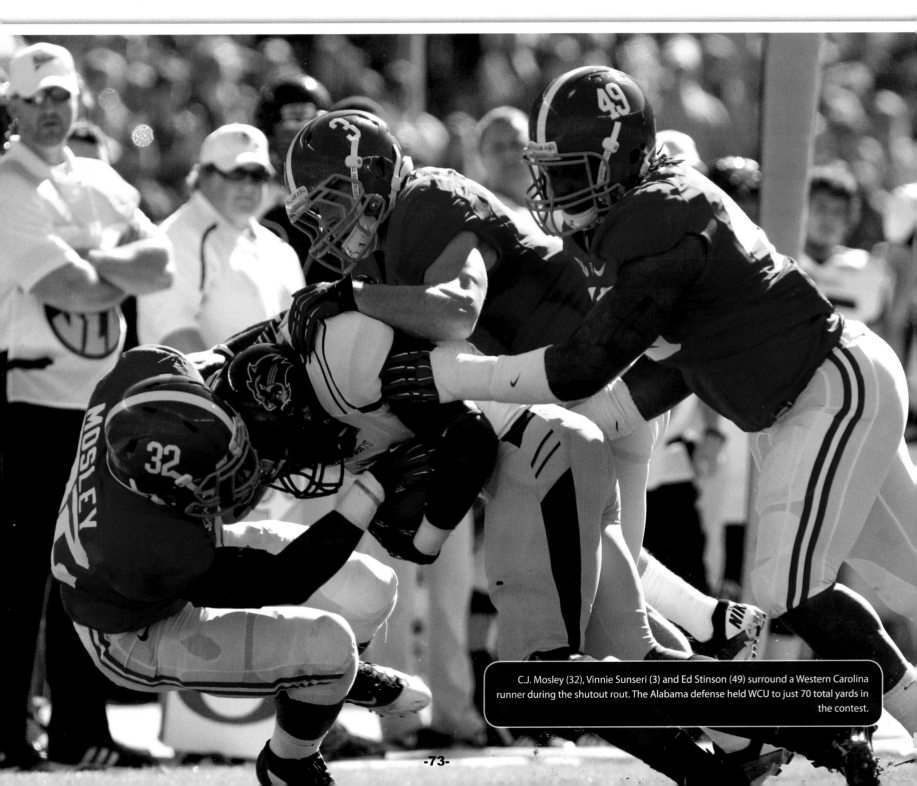

C.J. Mosley (32), Vinnie Sunseri (3) and Ed Stinson (49) surround a Western Carolina runner during the shutout rout. The Alabama defense held WCU to just 70 total yards in the contest.

Wide receiver Christion Jones (22) hauls in a 29-yard touchdown pass from A.J. McCarron in the second quarter.

ALABAMA
49

AUBURN
0

Auburn's 3-8 record coming into the annual Iron Bowl may have taken away some of the suspense from one of the nation's great rivalry games, but a win over the Tigers was all that stood between Alabama and an opportunity to play for the SEC title a week later in Atlanta. That was more than enough motivation for the No. 2-ranked Crimson Tide.

The sellout crowd at Bryant-Denny Stadium enjoyed the Crimson Tide's shutout victory over archrival Auburn.

(Above) Eddie Lacy (42) gets past Auburn's Daren Bates (25) during one of his 18 rushes for 131 yards and two touchdowns. (Opposite page, inset) Wide receiver Kevin Norwood (83) beats Auburn's Joshua Holsey (15) for a 38-yard TD catch in the third quarter.

Alabama's offense, led by quarterback A.J. McCarron, scored on its first seven possessions en route to a historic 49-0 rout of its cross-state rival. It was the second-most one-sided Iron Bowl game ever — and the largest margin since 1948, when the Tide won 55-0.

With the Senior Day victory, Alabama secured the SEC Western Division title and advanced to play Eastern champion Georgia in Atlanta's Georgia Dome. The stakes could not have been higher — the winner of that game would most likely play for the BCS National Championship in Miami on Jan. 7, 2013.

"Certainly when we're at our best, we're hard to beat," Tide senior center Barrett Jones said following his final game in Bryant-Denny Stadium. "I think we're playing on all cylinders right now."

It was also another big day for Alabama freshman wide receiver Amari Cooper, who had five catches for 109 yards and two touchdowns, including a 37-yard strike from McCarron, and a 29-yard catch and run through the Tiger defense into the end zone.

(Left) Amari Cooper (9) leaps to catch a pass from A.J. McCarron in front of Tigers cornerback Jonathon Mincy (6). Cooper caught a pair of TD passes as part of a five-reception, 109-yard game. (Inset) Safety Robert Lester (37) brings down an Auburn player. Lester had an interception in the rout.

Tide running back Eddie Lacy had one of his best games of the season, rushing for 131 yards on 18 carries and two touchdowns. Backups T.J. Yeldon and Kenyan Drake also had impressive rushing performances. Overall, Alabama had 483 total yards to just 163 for Auburn.

Paced by senior safety Robert Lester's five tackles and one interception, it was the Tide's fourth shutout of the season, the most in a single season by an Alabama team since 1979.

"I was really proud of the way our players competed in the game today," Alabama coach Nick Saban said. "I felt great about the seniors being able to close out their career here with a pretty memorable victory for them.

This is a great rivalry game, and for our players to be able to win this game is always a big thing for our fans, our players and all of our supporters."

Saban then turned his attention to Georgia.

"It's a great opportunity to play a really good team in the University of Georgia in the SEC Championship Game," he said. "To me, in all those games that I've been a part of, they are about as good as any game in the country other than the national championship game."

T.J. Yeldon (4) battles Auburn's T'Sharvan Bell (22). Yeldon had a 2-yard touchdown run in the first quarter.

The Alabama defense was all over the Tigers as Xzavier Dickson (47) and Damion Square (92) team up to stop an Auburn runner.

SEC CHAMPIONSHIP GAME
DEC. 1, 2012

ALABAMA
32

GEORGIA
28

The phrase "one for the ages" is often ov
it has never been more appropriate than
December evening inside the Georgia Dor
By the time the streamers fell from the ceiling a
of confetti blasted up from cannons on the field, A
captured its 23rd Southeastern Conference Ch
earning a date against old nemesis Notre Dame
BCS National Championship Game.

(Above) The Million Dollar Band spells out "BAMA" during a performance prior to th
Championship Game in A

Alabama's Amari Cooper (9) fights for extra yardage as Georgia's Damian Swann (5), Bacarri Rambo (18) and Alec Ogletree (9) surround him. Cooper had seven catches for 127 yards and the game-winning 45-yard touchdown catch with 3:15 remaining. (Opposite page) Eddie Lacy breaks free of the Georgia defense. Lacy rushed for 181 yards and a pair of TDs against the Bulldogs.

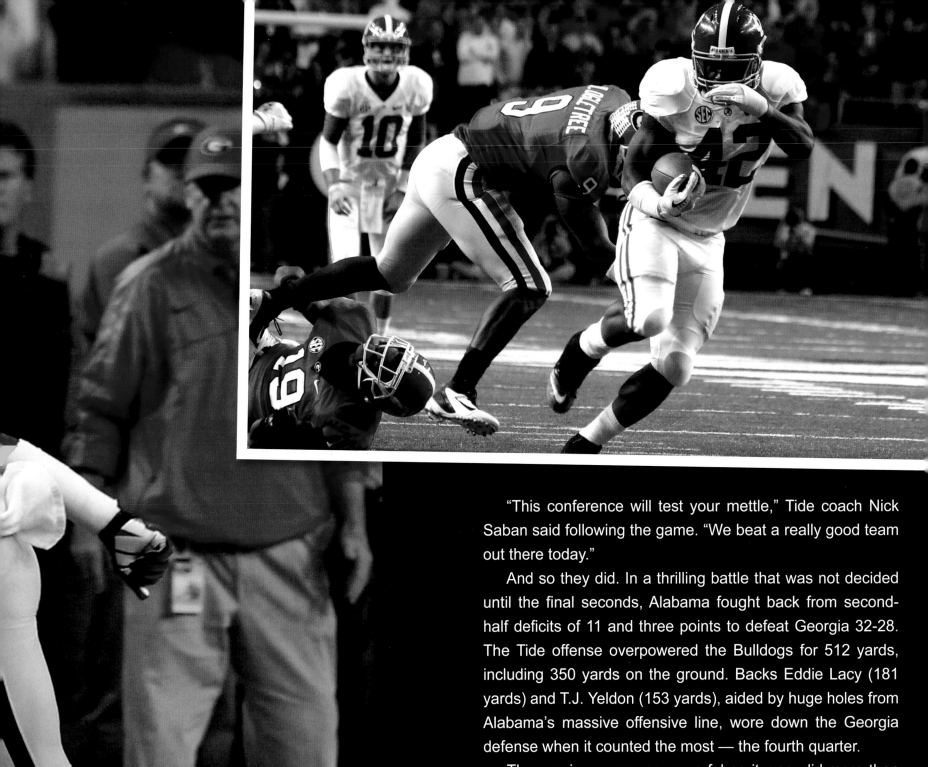

"This conference will test your mettle," Tide coach Nick Saban said following the game. "We beat a really good team out there today."

And so they did. In a thrilling battle that was not decided until the final seconds, Alabama fought back from second-half deficits of 11 and three points to defeat Georgia 32-28. The Tide offense overpowered the Bulldogs for 512 yards, including 350 yards on the ground. Backs Eddie Lacy (181 yards) and T.J. Yeldon (153 yards), aided by huge holes from Alabama's massive offensive line, wore down the Georgia defense when it counted the most — the fourth quarter.

The running game, as powerful as it was, did more than move the Tide up and down the field; it set up what would become the game-winning touchdown. With 3:23 remaining and behind 28-25, Alabama had first-and-10 from the Bulldog 45. Expecting another run or a short pass, Georgia defenders crowded the line. McCarron instead dropped back, faked a handoff to Yeldon and threw a perfect deep touchdown strike to Amari Cooper. The Tide's 32-28 lead would hold, but not without some tense moments for those in crimson and white.

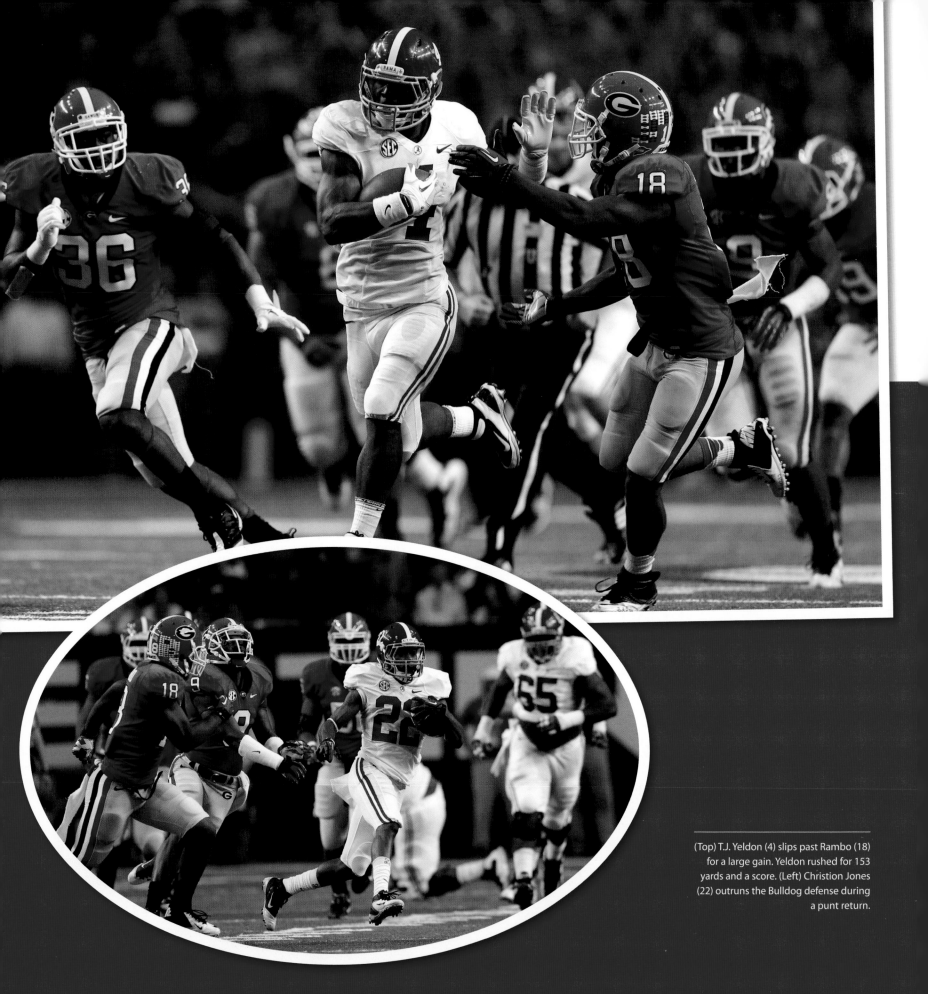

(Top) T.J. Yeldon (4) slips past Rambo (18) for a large gain. Yeldon rushed for 153 yards and a score. (Left) Christion Jones (22) outruns the Bulldog defense during a punt return.

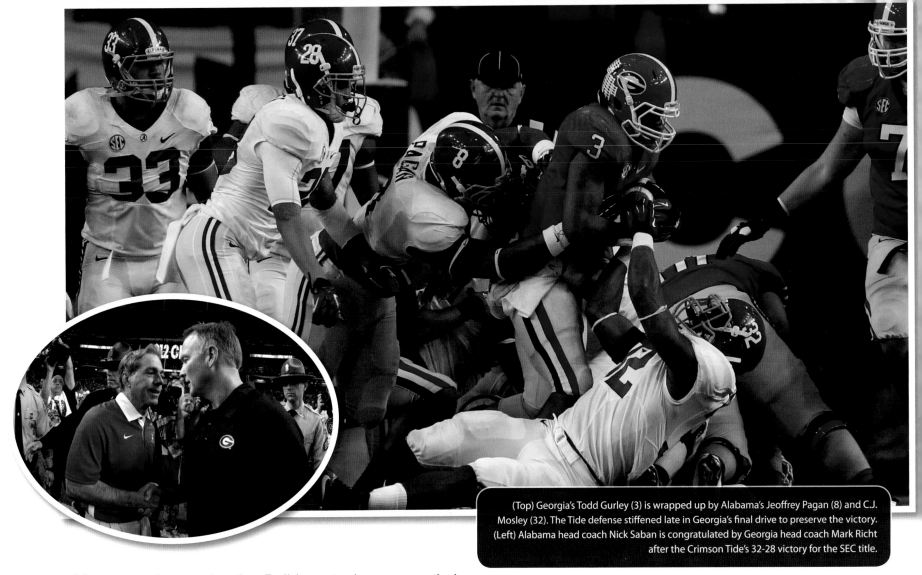

(Top) Georgia's Todd Gurley (3) is wrapped up by Alabama's Jeoffrey Pagan (8) and C.J. Mosley (32). The Tide defense stiffened late in Georgia's final drive to preserve the victory. (Left) Alabama head coach Nick Saban is congratulated by Georgia head coach Mark Richt after the Crimson Tide's 32-28 victory for the SEC title.

After swapping punts, the Bulldogs took over on their own 15-yard line with 1:08 to go and no timeouts remaining. After moving the ball to their 28 after a 9-yard pass and a 4-yard run, on first-and-10 quarterback Aaron Murray's downfield pass was tipped by Vinnie Sunseri and appeared to be intercepted by Alabama's Dee Milliner. Tide fans and players celebrated what looked like a game-ender. But after review, officials ruled the ball hit the ground, and Georgia had new life.

Murray then completed passes of 15 and 23 yards before hitting tight end Arthur Lynch on a 26-yarder to the Alabama 8. On first-and-goal, but with time running out, Murray chose not to spike the ball. Instead, his fade-route attempt was tipped at the line of scrimmage by C.J. Mosley on a delayed rush. The ball was caught by the Bulldogs' Chris Conley, but for a harmless 3-yard gain. As Georgia fans grimaced and Tide fans cheered, the clock counted down to zero.

Amidst the whirlwind last few minutes, Alabama's victory meant one thing — the Tide was headed to Miami to defend its BCS National Championship.

"This game is going to last a long time as one of the great SEC Championships," said freshman star Amari Cooper, who finished with seven receptions for 127 yards. "I'm glad I could be part of it."

Saban, 2-1 in SEC Championship games with Alabama, said, "We kind of had that, 'I would not be denied' attitude out there today. I'm not saying we played our best football game of the year in terms of execution, but the way we were able to run the ball, especially in the second half, was probably the difference in the game.

"I couldn't be prouder, not only for the way they competed in this game but for the way they have come back all year."

(Left) Saban and the Tide receive the SEC Championship Trophy in post-game ceremonies. Lacy (42) received the game's Most Outstanding Player award. (Bottom) The Alabama players carry around the "A" flag after the SEC title game.

JAN. 7, 2013

ALABAMA
42

NOTRE DAME
14

I t seemed inevitable. Even as Alabama fans celebrated a thrilling 32-28 Crimson Tide victory over Georgia in the SEC Championship Game, thoughts of an old nemesis took center stage.

Notre Dame.

Two words, one team and a bonfire of memories in the minds of older Alabama fans.

(Above) The Alabama defense was dominant in the BCS National Championship Game. The Tide's Geno Smith (24) and Deion Belue (13) wrap up Notre Dame's Cierre Wood (20).

To be sure, the Tide's win in Atlanta earned the team a third trip in four years to the Bowl Championship Series National Championship Game — an unprecedented feat. But this one was different. This was not the usual anticipation of BCS glory. This was a chance to revisit history.

Alabama versus Notre Dame.

No other BCS pairing could match this one, at least as far as longtime Crimson Tide fans were concerned. A matchup with the Oregon Ducks, for instance, would have had intense buzz and hype. Yet it still would not have risen to the level of meeting the Fighting Irish in Miami for the national championship. It's hard to compete with ghosts of the past.

Never mind that Alabama was the team that had won two BCS titles in three years and established itself as college football's premier program. By contrast, no players on either Alabama's or Notre Dame's roster had even been born the last time the Irish won a national title in 1988. But this was still Notre Dame, perhaps the only team in college football that could claim a more storied past than the Crimson Tide.

(Preceding page, left) Alabama's Eddie Lacy (42) breaks free of Notre Dame's KeiVarae Russell (6). (Above) Tide defenders C.J. Mosley (32), HaHa Clinton-Dix (6) and Dee Milliner (28) surround a Notre Dame ballcarrier.

(Top) Amari Cooper (9) gets help from Christion Jones (22) to gain extra yardage. Cooper led the Tide with six catches for 105 yards and two touchdowns. (Left) Trey DePriest (33) and Robert Lester (37) tackle a Fighting Irish player.

(Above) Alabama defensive end Quinton Dial (90) draws a bead on Notre Dame quarterback Everett Golson (5).

This was also the program that Alabama fans grew up to respect — and resent. There was the little matter of the 1966 season, when Kenny Stabler and the Tide went undefeated, untied, wiped out Nebraska 34-7 in the Sugar Bowl and still finished third in wire service polls behind Notre Dame and Michigan State, two Midwestern teams that famously played to a 10-10 tie.

Fast forward seven seasons to the 1973 Sugar Bowl, when Alabama had a chance to right the wrong, only to lose 24-23 in a classic first-ever head-to-head meeting with the Fighting Irish. Both teams went into the game undefeated, but only one, Notre Dame, emerged with a perfect record.

It only got worse for the Tide the following season when the Irish once again defeated an 11-0 Alabama team, this time by two points in the Orange Bowl. Two years later,

Nov. 13, 1976, the two teams met for a third time, this one in Notre Dame's home stadium in South Bend. The result seemed almost predictable: A three-point Irish victory.

"It's getting worse with age," said then-Alabama coach Paul "Bear" Bryant in a cramped visitor locker room after the 21-18 loss. "One, two and three points. I doubt that I'll make it to the four-pointer."

Bryant did, however, make it to that fourth game, held at Birmingham's Legion Field in 1980. And the Tide lost again, this time 7-0. Despite his legendary run as Alabama's coach, the fact that Bryant was 0-4 against the Irish was not lost on Tide fans even as they celebrated the 2012 SEC title in the Georgia Dome. They knew the rest of the team's history with Notre Dame, including Alabama's lone victory in the series — a 28-10 win in 1986 — followed by another loss in 1987.

That left Alabama with a 1-5 record against the Irish. Until Jan. 7, 2013, that is.

Getting less attention, however, in the 37 days between the Tide's victory over Georgia and the BCS national title showdown was the intense pressure building on Notre Dame. Not only were the Irish chasing their own history, they came into the game with the No. 1 ranking and a 12-0 record, one of only two undefeated major college teams. (The other, Ohio State, was not eligible for postseason play due to NCAA sanctions).

Three days before the BCS title game, Notre Dame wide receiver T.J. Jones summed up the challenge facing his team.

"I think now it has a lot to do with restoring Notre Dame to glory," Jones told reporters. "Last one was in '88. It's been a while. People expect Notre Dame to be great; they expect greatness of us."

This was the sort of intense national spotlight that the current group of Irish players had never experienced. Alabama, by contrast, had owned this stage in two of the three previous BCS title games.

Among the comments, analysis and predictions that became part of the massive pregame hype, Notre Dame's Jones once again said it well: "People always say that in order to be the best, you've got to beat the best. Alabama, just like Notre Dame, has been one of the best through history, and most recently they've been one of the best in about the last five years. So if we want to be the No. 1 team in the nation, and go undefeated, we have to beat an Alabama-caliber team."

The Alabama offense takes care of business up front as tight end Kelly Johnson (31), tackle Cyrus Kouandjio (71), tight end Michael Williams (89) and guard Chance Warmack (65) all execute their blocking assignments.

(Top) Lacy (42) eludes Notre Dame's Zeke Motta (17). (Right) Alabama director of strength and conditioning Scott Cochran exhorts the Tide between plays.

The Alabama offense huddles up to hear the play call from quarterback A.J. McCarron. The Tide offense rolled up 529 yards and six touchdowns in the rout of the Irish.

(Top) Lester (37) and Milliner (28) team up for a tackle. (Right) Center Barrett Jones (75) keeps an eye on Notre Dame's Dan Fox (48) and Kona Schwenke (96) after the snap.

The events of Monday night, Jan. 7, in a jam-packed Sun Life Stadium in Miami Gardens, Florida, proved just how much of a test Notre Dame faced. Not only were the Irish not used to the BCS limelight, their team — as their coach would later admit — was simply not at the same playing level as Alabama.

The difference in the teams was obvious from the opening series — a five-play, 82-yard Tide touchdown drive that shattered any pretense Notre Dame had the best defense in America. After all, the Irish had come into the game not only with the No. 1 ranking, but the No. 1 scoring defense as well. Before the night was over, Alabama, known for its stifling defensive teams under coach Nick Saban, would not only own the No. 1 title again, it would take the scoring defense title away from Notre Dame as well.

The Tide's opening drive was the longest the Irish had given up all season, but as the game unfolded, it turned out to be not even Alabama's longest one of the night. That belonged to a crushing 97-yard third-quarter march, one of six Tide touchdown drives. All told, Alabama's offense used drives of 82, 61, 80, 71, 97 and 86 yards to rout the Irish 42-14 before a record stadium crowd of 80,120 and nearly 30 million viewers watching on national television.

The resounding victory gave Alabama its third BCS national title in four years and left analysts searching for adequate superlatives to describe the domination. One word seemed obvious: "Dynasty."

"I guess you can call it what you want," Tide quarterback A.J. McCarron said in the locker room after the game. "I'm just happy to be part of this win right now."

McCarron (10) calls the signals as Anthony Steen gets set to block.

McCarron (10) rolls out to throw a pass. McCarron completed 20 of 28 passes for 264 yards and four touchdowns in the title game.

McCarron, who had been the most valuable offensive player in the Crimson Tide's 21-0 BCS title win over LSU a year earlier, had another stellar night on the BCS stage, completing 20 of 28 passes for 264 yards and four touchdowns.

Alabama became only the third team ever to win three titles in four years, and the first to accomplish the feat since Nebraska in the mid-1990s. In the BCS era, which began in 1998, the Tide stood alone with three championships.

With the win, Alabama had 61 victories in a five-year span dating back to 2008 — the most wins during a five-year span in college football history.

"Everything we wanted to accomplish, we've accomplished," said senior long snapper Carson Tinker, speaking for the most productive senior class in Crimson Tide history. "We stayed committed."

(Top) Milliner (28) makes a stop of an Irish ballcarrier. (Above) Mosley (32) makes one of his eight tackles in the BCS title game.

(Above) Saban directs the Tide during the BCS title game. (Right) Defensive coordinator Kirby Smart sends the signals in for the Crimson Tide.

Despite its role as the defending champion, Alabama was clearly the team that played like it had something to prove in South Florida. Notre Dame, led by Heisman Trophy runner-up Manti Te'o, a linebacker who would later become embroiled in a national controversy over an online girlfriend hoax, was simply overwhelmed.

The Tide rushed out to 28-0 halftime lead — such a dominant performance that even Irish coach Brian Kelly could do little but acknowledge the vast difference between the teams. Asked at halftime by an ESPN reporter what could be done to turn things around, Kelly candidly answered: "Maybe Alabama doesn't come back in the second half. It's all Alabama. I mean, we can't tackle them right now. Who knows why? They're big and physical."

Guard Anthony Steen (61) opens a hole through Notre Dame's Louis Nix III (9) for T.J. Yeldon (4) to run through as McCarron watches the play unfold. Yeldon rushed for 108 yards and a score against the Irish.

After the game, when Notre Dame's dream of bringing a national championship back to South Bend had been shattered, Kelly matter-of-factly said his team learned just how far of an expanse exists between getting to the title game and winning it against an elite SEC team. This was the seventh consecutive time an SEC team had won the national title.

"We've got to get physically stronger, continue to close the gap there, and just overall you need to see what it looks like," Kelly said. "Our guys clearly know what it looks like. When I say 'know what it looks like,' a championship football team. They're (Alabama) back-to-back national champs. So that's what it looks like."

(Above) Jesse Williams (54) fights through a Notre Dame blocker to get to Golson. (Left) Tight ends and special teams coach Bobby Williams gets the attention of his players.

Warmack (65) helps Yeldon (4) get through the Notre Dame defense.

McCarron (10) coolly looks for a receiver downfield as tackle D.J. Fluker (76) keeps the pocket clean.

Although the nation has become accustomed to watching Alabama dominate its opponents defensively, it was the Tide's offense that captured most of the postgame headlines.

Led by McCarron and a veteran offensive line, Alabama attacked Notre Dame's defense with a daunting assortment of skill players, including standout freshman wide receiver Amari Cooper and running backs Eddie Lacy and T.J. Yeldon. Lacy was named the game's most valuable offensive player following a performance of 157 all-purpose yards and two touchdowns. Yeldon added 108 rushing yards. Cooper, playing in his hometown, hauled in six receptions for 105 yards and two touchdowns.

Overall, the Tide totaled 529 yards to 302 for the Irish, with much of that coming after the outcome was decided in the second half.

"We came out, started fast and finished strong like we always preach," McCarron said.

Alabama linebacker C.J. Mosley was named the defensive player of the game for a solid performance that contributed to holding Notre Dame to just 32 yards rushing.

Yet, it was the Tide's offensive line that drew the most praise. Led by All-American center Barrett Jones, who played with torn ligaments in his left foot, Alabama overpowered Notre Dame's much-heralded defense. Te'o, who just weeks earlier had won more national awards than any defensive player in history, could be seen missing tackle after tackle when he wasn't being blocked straight up out of a play.

"It started in the locker room (before the game)," Tide offensive tackle D.J. Fluker said. "We had the mindset that we were going to come out here and dominate. We were all fired up today."

"We were surprised with how the score ended up, but we knew we would come out and dominate," said Barrett Jones.

The domination began soon after the opening kickoff. Alabama took less than three minutes to score, following runs from Lacy and a 29-yard pass from McCarron to Kevin Norwood. Lacy took it the final 20 yards into the end zone, and a Jeremy Shelley extra point made it 7-0.

The drive was the first sign of trouble for Notre Dame, which had given up just two rushing touchdowns in the red zone all season.

(Below) Yeldon (4) slips free of Notre Dame's Motta (17) as Jones (75) and Warmack (65) look on.

(Above) Michael Williams (89) looks the football into his hands for a touchdown catch.

(Left) McCarron (10) prepares to hand off to Lacy (42). (Below) The Alabama offense took apart the Notre Dame defense, led by Manti Te'o (5), as the Tide scored on six of its first eight possessions.

Minutes later, following a Notre Dame punt and a 15-yard penalty against the Irish for interfering with a fair catch, the Tide took over where it left off — owning the line of scrimmage. Alabama moved 61 yards in 10 plays, alternating between rushes from Lacy and short passes to Cooper and Marvin Shinn. A 3-yard touchdown pass from McCarron to tight end Michael Williams completed the drive. Shelley's extra point made it Alabama 14-0.

Minutes later, with the first quarter winding down, the Tide was back on the Irish goal line after long passes from McCarron to Norwood and Cooper. Yeldon's 1-yard plunge into the end zone just as the second quarter began capped an 80-yard drive. Another Shelley extra point made it 21-0.

(Right) Lacy (42) bulls his way for extra yards. He scored on a 20-yard run and an 11-yard catch in the game. (Bottom) Saban paces the Alabama sideline as his assistants keep an eye on the action.

(Below) Saban salutes the Alabama faithful after the Crimson Tide beat Notre Dame 42-14.

Yet another Alabama touchdown just before halftime seemed to seal the outcome. After runs by Yeldon, and a 27-yard strike from McCarron to Christion Jones, the Tide had a first down on Notre Dame's 11-yard line with under a minute left in the half. McCarron dropped back, threw a short pass over the middle to Lacy, and the running back used two jaw-dropping spin moves to get into the end zone. A Shelley extra point made it 28-0.

"I feel like the game changed at halftime, or right before halftime," McCarron said. "The touchdown pass to Eddie, when he bounced off two guys and put it in. I think that kind of took the life out of them."

The only question left was whether Alabama would complete another BCS title game shutout, as it did a year earlier against LSU. Notre Dame answered that question with two second-half touchdowns, largely because of the passing of quarterback Everett Golson. Yet, the outcome was never in doubt — certainly not after the Tide's 10-play, 97-yard scoring drive on the first series of the second half.

The long drive began after Alabama safety HaHa Clinton-Dix made a diving interception at the Tide 3-yard line as soon as the ball was tipped by teammate Dee Milliner.

McCarron and Saban wade through a throng of media to conduct interviews after the Crimson Tide's BCS title victory.

Mosley holds up both the crystal football and his trophy as the defensive Most Outstanding Player of the 2013 BCS National Championship Game. Mosley led the Tide with eight tackles.

Alabama quickly marched down the field, alternating between runs by Lacy and Yeldon and receptions from Norwood and Christion Jones. With a first down at Notre Dame's 34-yard line, McCarron dropped back and threw to a wide-open Cooper down the sideline for a touchdown.

The Tide was up 35-0 before the Irish finally scored late in the third quarter, ending Alabama's streak of more than 108 minutes in BCS title games without giving up a point. That streak included an unanswered run of 69 consecutive points by the Tide, dating back to the fourth quarter of the 2010 BCS title game against Texas.

Alabama added its final touchdown, another pass from McCarron to Cooper, this one for 19 yards, with under 12 minutes left in the fourth quarter.

Down 42-7, Notre Dame mounted a final 75-yard scoring drive, including a 6-yard touchdown pass from Golson to running back Theo Riddick.

The drama, however, wasn't over. Up 42-14 with 7:03 left in the game, McCarron and Barrett Jones got into a play-call dispute as time ticked down on the play clock. McCarron yelled at Jones, who responded forcefully by pushing his quarterback back a couple of yards. As many analysts later joked, it was the only real hit McCarron took all night.

Minutes later, the two teammates put it behind them.

"As soon as it happened, we let it go," McCarron said. "He takes care of me. I take care of him. We really are best friends."

The spat, with the game's outcome already decided, underscored just how focused the Tide was for this game, and impressed at least one sports superstar — the Los Angeles Lakers' Kobe Bryant.

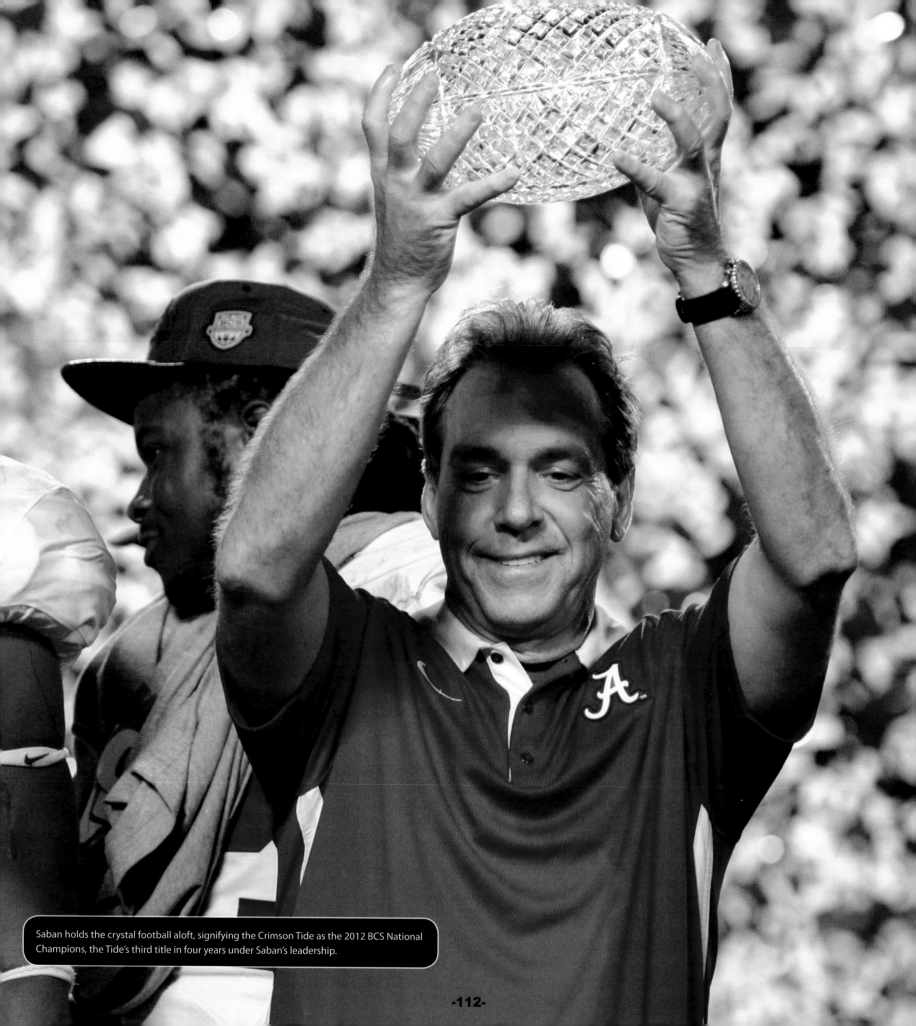

Saban holds the crystal football aloft, signifying the Crimson Tide as the 2012 BCS National Champions, the Tide's third title in four years under Saban's leadership.

Saban and Mosley speak to the assembled media after the BCS title game.

"We just saw why bama will be bcs champs @10AJMcCarron and @barrettAjones not afraid to confront each other in order to win. #respect," Bryant tweeted.

Following the game, as the D-word, "Dynasty," became synonymous with Alabama, Saban put it in perspective.

"I don't think words like 'dynasty' are really words that I'm much interested in," he said. "You know, we're interested in accomplishment and consistency in performance, and we want to continue to try to do that in the future. So those (words) are for other people to talk about."

But one thing seemed certain: Dynasty or not, whatever ghosts lingered from those long-ago losses to Notre Dame disappeared on a magical night in South Florida.

"I think it's pretty special what we've accomplished, what the players accomplished, what the coaches accomplished," Saban said. "And one of these days when I'm sitting on the side of a hill watching the stream go by, I'll probably figure it out even more. But what about next year's team? You've got to think about that, too."

THE COACHES' TROP[HY]

THE AMERICAN FOOTBALL COACHES ASSOCIATION®
FOUNDED 1922

THE NATIONAL CHAMPION

UNIVERSITY OF ALABAMA 2012

USA TODAY TOP 25 COACHES' POLL

BCS
BOWL CHAMPIONSHIP SERIES

PRESENTED BY

Dr Pepper

(Opposite page and above) Moore, Bonner, Terry Saban and Mosley look on as Coach Saban speaks to ESPN's John Saunders after Alabama's victory.

(Opposite page and left) The confetti flies in South Florida's Sun Life Stadium after Alabama was awarded the The Coaches Trophy, signifying the Tide's 15th national championship. (Above) Lacy, who was named the game's offensive Most Outstanding Player after rushing for 140 yards and one score and catching a TD pass, holds the championship crystal.

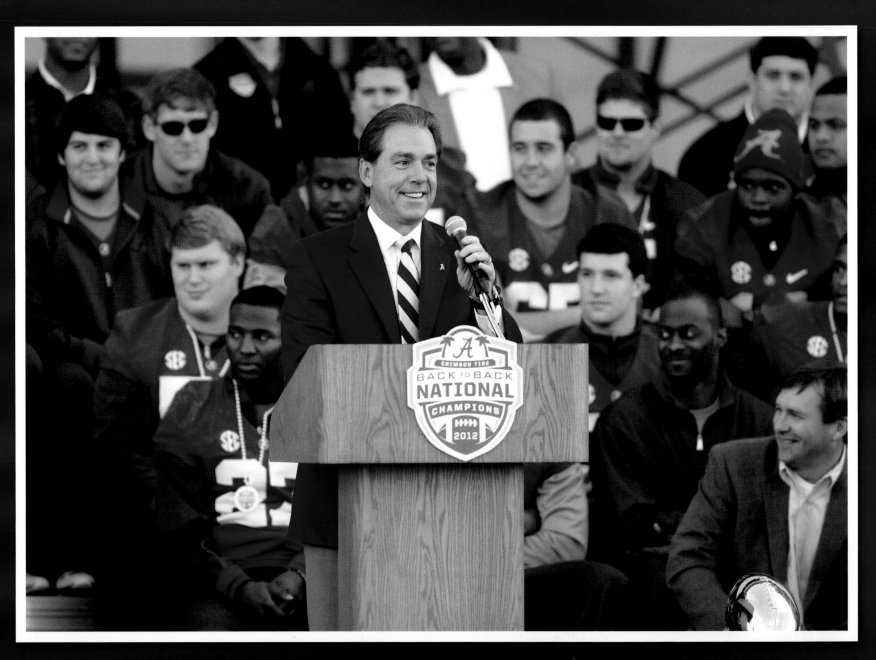

(Opposite page) Saban and the Crimson Tide celebrate their 15th national title on the steps of Bryant-Denny Stadium. (Above left) Moore and Bonner ride in the championship parade in Tuscaloosa. (Above right) The Sabans enjoy the parade festivities. (Left) Crimson Tide players hand out commemorative footballs to fans during the parade. (Below) The Alabama spirit squads and the Million Dollar Band march along the parade route.

BCS NATIONAL CHAMPI

The Birmingham N

BAMA

BCS NATIONAL CHAMPIONS

The Birmingham News

BAMA AGAIN!

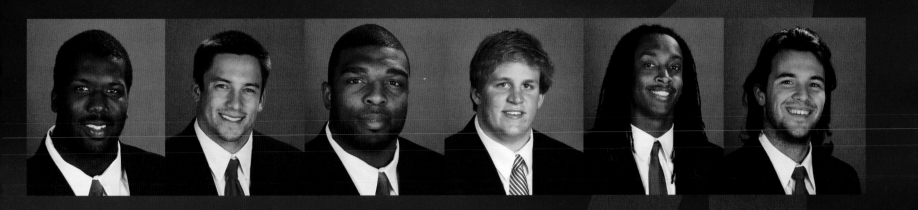

THE STAR SENIORS

The University of Alabama football team won its 15th national title in the program's storied history by defeating Notre Dame in the 2013 BCS National Championship Game. Leading the Crimson Tide to its second consecutive national title, and three of the last four BCS championships, were 11 seniors who accomplished more in their collegiate careers than any other players in the history of the game.

QUINTON DIAL #90

Three weeks before playing in the BCS National Championship Game on Jan. 7, 2013, defensive end Quinton Dial graduated from the University of Alabama. A college diploma is significant in anyone's life, but for Dial, it had even more meaning.

It was part of a commitment he made when he joined the Crimson Tide as a junior-college transfer in January 2011. An academic transcript had ultimately cost him a chance to play for Alabama two years earlier.

Now, he made the most of a second chance, both on and off the field.

"You've got to graduate," said Dial. "After football, you have to ask yourself, 'what are you going to do now?' You can't play football anymore. You have to have self-discipline."

The 6-foot-6, 300-pound lineman leaves Alabama not only with a diploma, but also with a record of 46 tackles over two years, including eight for loss, and 2.5 sacks. These might not seem like earthshaking numbers, but more importantly, Dial's containment ability frustrated opposing offenses, as did his penchant for stuffing the run and jamming up blockers for the Tide's linebackers to make plays on the ball.

"It was a great time," said Dial. "I loved being with these guys every step of the way. I wouldn't trade it for anything."

Originally a 2009 Alabama signee, Dial had been named the Alabama High School Athletic Association's 2008 Class 6A Lineman of the Year following his senior season at Clay-Chalkville High School in Pinson.

Quinton Dial (90) tackles Notre Dame running back Theo Riddick during the Crimson Tide's 2013 BCS National Championship Game rout of the Fighting Irish.

Dial, wrapping up Riddick in the BCS title game, had 22 total tackles during the 2012 season.

Ironically, Dial hadn't even started playing football until his freshman year in high school — the same year, he said, that a poor academic performance affected his transcript and ultimately cost him a place on the 2009 Alabama team.

"I wasn't a football fan growing up," he said. "I didn't really follow it. I didn't get into football until my freshman year when the high school coach told me he thought I could have a future in it."

That proved to be an understatement. By the time he finished his senior season at Clay-Chalkville, Rivals.com rated Dial the No. 33 high school defensive tackle in the nation.

When he failed to qualify academically at Alabama, Dial opted to play the next two seasons at East Mississippi Community College before rejoining the Crimson Tide in 2011. He wasted no time in making an impact on the Tide's defensive line, with significant playing time in 12 games in 2011 and all 14 in 2012.

Having won a national title in 2011, the 2012 team entered the season with major personnel losses on defense to the NFL, but Dial said he and his teammates were determined to carry on the legacy.

"Going into the Michigan game, we had a chip on our shoulder because the media was talking about how we lost Dont'a (Hightower), Mark Barron, Courtney Upshaw and others," he said. "We had to perform because we wanted to be better than that group. That was just how we came out and played every week."

Ultimately, like the 2011 team, the 2012 version also finished No. 1 in the nation in scoring defense, total defense and rushing defense, among other categories.

"Back in the offseason, we all had team affirmations and said that we wanted to be there in January, playing on the biggest stage in college football," said Dial. "So we got everybody buying into the system that Coach Saban set up. We got a group of men seeing the same vision."

Asked about the 2012 team's ability to pick up where the more veteran 2011 team left off, Saban told reporters a day before the BCS title game in Miami, "To be honest, I think this team has kind of exceeded expectations. If you look at all the players that we lost last year, the leadership that we lost, the injuries we've had, the schedule that we played, the adversity they had to overcome, the new roles that so many people had on this team … I'm really proud of what this team actually was able to accomplish together as a group."

Soft-spoken off the field, Dial speaks modestly about his own role in contributing to two back-to-back national championships and a SEC title. Part of that, he said, comes from the knowledge that arrogance doesn't translate into winning.

"Staying hungry and humble is important," Dial said. "If you're not humble, then you become complacent, and it shows up on the field that you're not playing to the standard that we set at Alabama."

And it goes well beyond the play on the field, he said. It's a hallmark of Saban's "Process" at Alabama.

"You're representing this university, your family and the football team," said Dial. "Coach Saban wants everybody to represent it in a first-class way, to be smart about how you go about things when you're not at the university, when you're away from it."

Dial expects to play at the next level in the NFL. But among the victories in which he contributed at Alabama, he said one in particular will stay with him — the come-from-behind 21-17 win at LSU on Nov. 3, 2012.

"We faced so much adversity in that game," said Dial. "We got down pretty quick in that game and showed the mental toughness that we had to come back and fight for it, and win that ballgame at LSU. They say you're not supposed to win at Death Valley. That'll be one of my favorite games of all time."

Dial locks up with Georgia offensive lineman Chris Burnette during the 2012 SEC Championship Game in Atlanta. The Tide beat the Bulldogs 32-28 in a game that saw three lead changes in the final quarter.

Although the Tide lost a week later to Texas A&M, the game served far more as motivation than anything else, according to Dial.

"We had to overcome," he said. "We knew the Texas A&M loss wasn't going to define our season."

As he prepares for the NFL, Dial has taken up a new hobby, something even most of his former Alabama teammates may not know.

"I'm learning to play the acoustic guitar," he said with a smile.

Asked if he sings, too, he said simply: "I do a little something, a little something. Always gotta have a backup plan, right?"

KELLY JOHNSON #31

Kelly Johnson (31) works to get free of a Notre Dame defender as Irish cornerback KeiVarae Russell (6) looks to get in Johnson's way during the BCS National Championship Game.

Kelly Johnson never received a football scholarship in his five years at the University of Alabama. Yet, as an H-back and tight end who played in all 14 of the Crimson Tide's games in 2012 and nine in 2011, he contributed significantly to Alabama's back-to-back national championship seasons.

"We didn't expect to win those back to back, or the three out of four years," said Johnson. "No one is going to hand you a championship. We had the mindset of 'Trust the coach' (Nick Saban). He's done it before. We believed in what he told us. We knew what we were there to do."

At 6-foot-3, 230 pounds, Johnson finished his senior year with five catches for 39 yards, including one reception in the BCS National Championship Game against Notre Dame. But his role was far more as a blocker for the Tide's high-profile running backs, most notably Eddie Lacy and T.J. Yeldon.

Speaking for others who battled in the trenches, Johnson said, "We don't mind being in the shadows. We're just doing our job. We like to get our hands dirty."

A Charlotte, North Carolina, native, Johnson walked on in 2008 to begin what would become an uphill struggle to play for the Crimson Tide.

"My father and I had been following Coach Saban for a long time," said Johnson. "I knew he was down there, and I just fell in love with the school when I went to visit."

But Kelly deferred his dreams of going beyond the scout team and getting on the field during games when he left the team in 2010, not sure what his future would be in Tuscaloosa. He found the answers soon enough.

"I wasn't satisfied with what I was doing," he said. "So I sat out a year and rearranged my thoughts, got refocused, came back and just settled in there and tried to carry the water until I got what I want."

Looking back now, with the hindsight of a veteran player, Johnson said he wouldn't trade anything for the experience. He credits tight ends coach Bobby Williams and strength and conditioning coach Scott Cochran, among others, for keeping him focused. Most of all, he said he respects Saban for helping him build the mental toughness needed to overcome all challenges, and leading by example.

"When I first walked into the locker room, it was the hardest thing ever to play for Coach Saban," said Johnson, referring to the high standards set by Alabama's head man. "Throughout the years, I just recognized that you're accountable. Every day you've got to show up and do what you're supposed to do, and do the job right and do it well. The biggest thing is accountability and your passion to play.

"It's about consistency," he added. "It's not just when you walk into the football building, but it's when you go home, when you go to class. What you do on campus."

Johnson said it helps that football is not just something players focus on during practice, in games or in the offseason at Alabama, but is "a lifestyle."

"There is no time off," he said. "That's how you win football games. If your goals aren't right, if you're not set on playing in that final (BCS title) game, you need to readjust yourself, take a look in the mirror and see what you want."

Although he leaves Alabama as one of the team's most celebrated walk-ons, Johnson hopes to continue his dream of playing in the NFL. To that extent, he was chosen as a team captain in the inaugural Raycom College Football All-Star Classic in Montgomery on Jan. 19, 2013, and received significant playing time during the game.

Nevertheless, whether he ends up in the NFL or not, Johnson said the experience with the Crimson Tide will stay with him for a lifetime.

"After running through that tunnel at Alabama, there are no regrets," he said.

And who knows? There's always another career on the horizon.

"My secret dream is to be a country music singer," Johnson said with a laugh. "I sing really loud in the shower and on car trips home."

(Preceding page) Johnson heads upfield as Mississippi State defensive back Darius Slay moves in to try to make a tackle during the Tide's 38-7 home victory over the Bulldogs. Johnson caught five passes for 39 yards during the 2012 season.

NICO JOHNSON #35

Like his Crimson Tide senior teammates, linebacker Nico Johnson will leave the University of Alabama with three national championship rings. Next up is what many consider a promising career in the NFL.

For Johnson, however, a more long-term goal was on his mind as he prepared to complete his studies for a criminal justice degree. Getting his diploma is not only something he promised his mother before her death in 2010, it is also a means to a very interesting end.

"I want to be an FBI agent one day," said Johnson. "So that's one thing I'm going to try to pursue, no matter how long it takes. Criminal justice has been fun for me, and I've enjoyed it throughout my whole college career."

Yet, given Johnson's penchant for tracking down opposing running backs, quarterbacks and receivers, the FBI will have to wait its turn for the services of the 6-foot-3, 245-pound middle linebacker.

A three-year starter in the Tide's base 3-4 defense, Johnson finished his senior season with 55 tackles and another national title. He was part of a senior class that set a SEC record of 49 wins in four years, and broke the national record previously held by Nebraska at 60 games.

"This same class has left a mark on history and the University of Alabama for years to come, when we're dead and gone," said Johnson. "Words can't explain how much it means to us to leave our legacy here at the University of Alabama."

Although Johnson said he initially agreed — following the Crimson Tide's 42-14 rout of Notre Dame in the BCS title game in January — with the "dynasty" word the media was labeling his team, he's now had time to reflect, and has changed his opinion.

"Sitting back after everything has calmed down, I really don't think it's a dynasty," said Johnson. "You know, Coach Saban's thing is he wants to go out every year and take advantage of the opportunity that the team has at hand, to go out and win another national championship. In years to come if he keeps winning, then yes, it's pretty much going to be called a 'dynasty.'"

Johnson expects his underclassmen to continue the legacy he and his teammates have left at Alabama. But the NFL now beckons, and he gives much of the credit to Saban and the Crimson Tide program.

"Being able to come through this program ... an almost-perfect NFL-style defense kind of prepares me better than if I would have gone anywhere else," he said.

Johnson called Saban "one of the greatest leaders I've known" and added, "I tried to learn a lot from him throughout my last year, trying to pick up as many things as I can. But he's that type of leader that his actions are his thing. He wants somebody to go out and do it. Don't sit back and say it; go out and do it."

"... an almost-perfect NFL-style defense kind of prepares me better than if I would have gone anywhere else."

— Nico Johnson

Johnson also credits Alabama strength and conditioning coach Scott Cochran for helping him get through the toughest time in his life. Johnson's mother, Mamie, died in June 2010 from complications of diabetes.

"A lot of people don't know that I was ready to give up football," said Johnson. "I was ready to be done and just focus on my degree because I was so emotionally drained and everything. But Coach Cochran, he kept me motivated, kept me understanding that life is not over because of a death. And I kind of understood that."

Asked prior to the NFL Draft where he would like to play in the NFL if it were up to him, Johnson singled out the Baltimore Ravens — not only because two of his former teammates (Courtney Upshaw and Terrence Cody) are on the team, but also because of the legacy left by retiring All-Pro linebacker Ray Lewis.

"Ray Lewis, he's my idol," said Johnson. "I've watched Ray Lewis throughout my whole high school career, from eighth grade on. He's that guy for me."

Johnson said he will give it everything he's got, no matter which team he plays for as a professional. And he has a bit of advice for the new Alabama recruits, some of whom will someday have the same opportunity to play in the NFL.

"Don't worry about trying to live up to the hype that Rivals.com created for you and all the websites in high school created for you," he said. "Just go out and be the best player you can be. And understand that you're going to make mistakes because it's something new. Just run with it."

(Right) Nico Johnson takes aim at Mississippi State quarterback Tyler Russell. (Opposite page) Johnson lines up against Notre Dame in the BCS National Championship Game. Johnson had 55 total tackles and two forced fumbles during the 2012 season.

BARRETT JONES #75

Crafting into just a few hundred words the career of Barrett Jones — perhaps the most decorated player in Alabama football history — is akin to reading a four-sentence review of Tolkien's *Lord of the Rings*. It could be done, but it wouldn't tell the whole story.

Jones' achievements, on and off the field, include:

- First-team all-state selection and a 2007 U.S. Army All-American from Evangelical Christian High School in Memphis, Tennessee.
- Freshman All-American at Alabama in 2009; starting right guard for all 14 games; Academic All-American; BCS National Championship No. 1.
- Starting right guard for 11 games in 2010; helped pave the way for Alabama's first Heisman Trophy winner, Mark Ingram; Academic All-American.
- Starting left tackle for 11 games in 2011; unanimous All-American; Outland Trophy winner as nation's best interior lineman; Jacobs Blocking Trophy winner as the SEC's top offensive lineman; Wuerffel Trophy winner for exemplary community service with athletic and academic achievement; Academic All-American; BCS National Championship No. 2.
- Starting center for 14 games in 2012; consensus All-American; Rimington Trophy winner as nation's best center; William V. Campbell Award, also known as the "Academic Heisman"; CoSIDA/Capital One Academic All-American of the Year; BCS National Championship No. 3.

To Jones, though, all the accolades are not important.

"If I'm known as Barrett Jones, a great Alabama football player, then I'm not doing my job," he said. "I want to be known as a Christian who happens to play football, not a football player who happens to be a Christian."

And so it is with Jones, the 6-foot-5, 305-pound do-it-all lineman extraordinaire whose faith is absolutely, positively the most important thing in his life. Not only does he talk the talk, he walks the walk, as evidenced by his three straight spring-break trips to the mission field.

Barrett Jones gets in blocking position after snapping the ball at LSU. Jones left Alabama as one of the most-decorated players in Tide history.

Just a few months following the January 2010 7.0 earthquake in Haiti, which killed an estimated 316,000 and left 1 million homeless, Jones traveled with a mission team from Memphis, and in Haiti he built showers, played games with the kids and showed that despite their tragedy, there were people who loved them.

The next year — only a few days after the Crimson Tide was honored by President Barack Obama at the White House — Jones returned to Haiti with 13 Alabama classmates and his family to help build a school and an orphanage, and to feed the hungry.

During the 2012 spring break, instead of going to the beach, he not only went to Nicaragua to minister to kids, but he planned most of the trip for 31 people.

"I've been to the beach a lot," said Jones, "but I don't really remember one particular trip. I remember the sand and the pool, but that's about it. Mission trips like these are different. They really make an impact on your life and you remember them forever."

Growing up just outside Memphis in Germantown — between his and his brothers' violin performances, school and church activities, and even a top-15 finish in a national Scrabble contest — Jones' storied football career began in the sixth grade. In his first game, his small private school lost badly to a larger public school, and his parents, Rex and Leslie Jones, thought for sure he would come back discouraged. Not so.

"My mom says I came back and said, 'I was born to play football!'" said Jones, who was also a basketball all-region player. "I loved football so much. The games were just so fun to me."

Jones being such a talented athlete didn't come as a surprise. His father played basketball for Alabama from 1981-84 under coach Wimp Sanderson. His grandfather, the legendary Bill Jones, was head basketball coach at North Alabama from 1974-86 and led his Lions to the Division II national championship in 1979.

Although an Alabama fan growing up, Jones' trek to Tuscaloosa was not a given.

"I was an Alabama fan, but I was by no means automatically coming here," said Jones. "I looked around at several other schools. And, to be honest, I probably wouldn't have come here had Coach Saban not been hired the year before. Once he started recruiting me and sat me down and gave me his vision for the program, then I really knew Alabama was where I wanted to go."

In fall 2008, Jones joined a star-studded class that included Mark Barron, Terrence Cody, Marcel Dareus, Jerrell Harris, Dont'a Hightower, Mark Ingram, Julio Jones, Robert Lester, Brad Smelley, Damion Square, Carson Tinker, Courtney Upshaw and Michael Williams. Of this group, eight became first-team All-Americans and seven were first-round NFL Draft picks.

"After my first few days hanging out with this class, I knew it was going to be something special," said Jones. "We had a lot of guys who were really committed to changing the culture

in the program and changing what people thought when they heard the name 'Alabama.' And, to an extent, I think we did that."

Jones and his class definitely "did that." During his five years (including his redshirt season in 2008), Alabama's 61 wins broke Nebraska's national record of 60, set from 1993-97. Jones credits Alabama's dominance during that time (two SEC titles and three BCS National Championships) to one man — Nick Saban — and his well-known "Process."

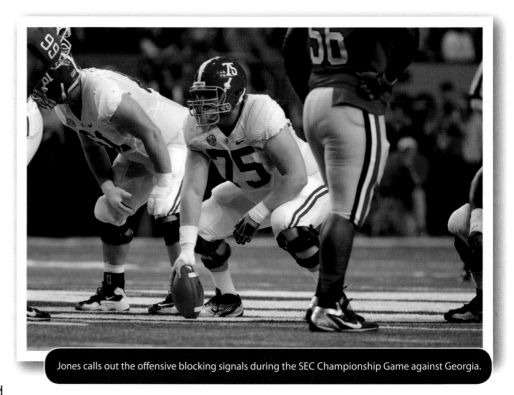
Jones calls out the offensive blocking signals during the SEC Championship Game against Georgia.

"Coach Saban has an awesome recipe, and if you follow the recipe, then it's going to work out for you," said Jones. "The 'Process' he talks about focuses on doing the little things right and not focusing on the results. It includes principles such as comparing yourself to a standard and not to others.

"But, it requires all the players to buy in to it. When coach first got here, he had to dismiss a few guys, but he had to do that to get everyone's attention."

Jones feels "The Process" has benefited him far beyond the football field.

"I've found the things Coach Saban teaches are helping me in other parts of life," said Jones. "I find myself thinking that way and using those things in school and in all sorts of things. Those principles aren't just football principles; they're life principles. I feel much better prepared for the world now that I've played for him."

Saban's sentiments toward Jones are similar.

"Barrett Jones is probably as fine a person, in terms of his leadership, his example that he sets, and the willingness that he has to serve other people with his time," said Saban. "He's one of the best students I've ever had the opportunity to coach, relative to his grade-point average and how successfully he is academically.

"I don't know if I've ever been around a guy that can play every position on the offensive line and do it efficiently, and win awards for all of those and still be as good of a person, as humble of a person, have as much humility as you could ever ask anyone and be very thoughtful of others," Saban continued. "There are just not very many people like him. He's special."

At no point in Jones' career did his "specialness" stand out more than in the Tide's thrilling 32-28 win over Georgia in the 2012 SEC Championship Game.

"Toward the end of the first quarter, as I was making a block, everything in the middle of my foot just popped and tore," Jones said. "I told the doctors at halftime that I had sprained my foot a little bit. But I knew it was something much worse than a sprain. It was probably the most pain I've ever had in a game."

Despite the seriousness of the injury — later diagnosed as a Lisfranc (middle foot) ligament tear — Jones toughed it out and never missed a play at center, helping backs Eddie Lacy and T.J. Yeldon lead the powerful Alabama running game to a whopping 350 yards against the Bulldogs.

The next evening at the year-end football awards banquet, Saban announced that Jones — along with Chance Warmack and Damion Square — had been elected a permanent team captain.

"That may be the biggest award I've ever received," said Jones, "because it's elected by your teammates. It's something that I'm very proud of."

During the lengthy layoff between the Georgia game and the BCS National Championship Game against Notre Dame, while Jones' Alabama teammates practiced, he rehabbed with swimming, biking and light jogging. Jones was determined to end his Tide career on the field, not as an observer.

"They would have had to physically drag me off the field to keep me from playing in the game," said Jones, who, because of his injury, had to develop a new blocking technique against Notre Dame's massive 330-pound nose guard, Louis Nix III. "I just didn't have much power in that foot."

With Jones back on the field almost the entire game, the Alabama offense rolled to its most balanced performance of the year — 265 yards rushing and 264 yards passing — in its 42-14 domination of the Fighting Irish. From the very first series, it was obvious to the record crowd in Miami Gardens' Sun Life Stadium and a national TV audience of almost 30 million that the Tide was light years ahead of Notre Dame in every phase of the game.

"I didn't play great, but I played all right and well enough to win," said a humble Jones. "Before the game, I felt like everyone was relaxed and confident. We had worked really hard and had a great week of practice. I think we definitely played our best game of the year."

Jones, who in four-and-a-half years earned undergraduate and master's degrees in accounting with a perfect 4.0 grade-point average, is leaving the door wide open on his future.

"I've come to realize that football is great, but it can't satisfy you," said Jones. "And if you look for your satisfaction and identity in football, then you're going to come up feeling empty.

"I think a big reason that God has allowed me to have so much success is because it's given me such a tremendous platform that opens doors and allows me to share my faith with other people.

"My faith is just not another thing that I do, it's who I am. It is my identity."

ROBERT LESTER #37

For Robert Lester, an Alabama career that ultimately would lead to three national championships in four years began quietly enough behind the scenes, in the tall shadow cast by a legendary high school teammate.

"You know, I went to school with Julio (Jones)," said Lester. "And he played on the opposite side of the ball. So, it gave me a chance to go out and compete against somebody that had extremely good talent."

Jones, now a standout wide receiver for the NFL's Atlanta Falcons, was on just about every college's recruiting list in the fall of 2007, when he and Lester, a defensive back, played together at Alabama's Foley High School.

College recruiters rushed to south Alabama to watch Jones, who was rated a five-star recruit and the top receiver prospect in the nation. But once there, they couldn't help but notice Lester, particularly when watching the teammates go against each other in practice.

"Everyone looked at Julio," said Lester, "and you know, I think I was rated a three-star. And when they came in and saw him, they'd see me on the opposite side going against him, and that's how I got a lot of attention and offers."

The rest, as they say, is Alabama football history. Both Jones and Lester signed with the Crimson Tide. While Jones started immediately, earning SEC Freshman of the Year honors, and later became an early first-round NFL Draft choice after his junior season, Lester was redshirted his freshman year and ended up spending five seasons at Alabama.

Lester and teammate Dee Milliner (28) wrap up Irish wide receiver DaVaris Daniels during the BCS title game. Lester had six tackles in the game.

It was a five-year span, however, in which the Crimson Tide won more games (61) than any college football team in history. And Lester, who started 40 of those games in the defensive backfield, became a huge part of the team's success. As it worked out, Lester ended his career with three national title rings, compared to one for his more famous high school teammate, Jones.

"After a while, it kind of got to the point to where we expected to win," said Lester. "The credit goes to Coach Saban for bringing in great guys, guys with great character, and believing in those guys to turn this program around."

Lester ended his career at Alabama tied for fifth on the team's all-time interception list with 14. That included two key interceptions (along with seven tackles) in a classic 24-20 come-from-behind victory over Arkansas in 2010, a game Lester considers his best at Alabama. His second interception, in particular, in the third quarter, stopped an Arkansas drive and gave Alabama a chance to take the lead. He was named SEC Defensive Player of the Week following the game.

"That's something I'll never forget," he said.

The Arkansas game, and the many that would follow, sealed Lester's role as one of the Crimson Tide's all-time defensive leaders. The team built such a reputation for its shutdown, dominating defense over Lester's career that a 2012 *New York Times* headline summed up the feelings of most players: "Crimson Tide's Defense Fears Only One Man: Saban."

Lester can attest to that.

"When I first got to Alabama, I thought Coach Saban hated me," said Lester. "I didn't think I was going to ever have a chance to play here. And as I grew up and matured, which he was pretty much helping me do by the tough coaching, he was getting me ready for what I needed to be ready for. I didn't realize it until I became a starter, which in his eyes was the time I was ready."

Saban made it clear following the Tide's 42-14 rout of Notre Dame in the BCS title game that players like Lester, who bought fully into his program, could take pride in their accomplishments years into the future.

"I mean, every player that's played for Alabama for the last six years since I've been there all deserve a lot of credit for this, and a lot of those guys came to Alabama when we weren't any good," said Saban. "I was getting killed down here. My credibility wasn't much. So they believed in the program and believed in what we could accomplish, and because those players came to Alabama, we've had a lot of success."

In that win over Notre Dame, Lester recorded six tackles and walked off the Sun Life Stadium field in South Florida satisfied that he and his teammates had not only left a legacy, but a benchmark for those who will follow them.

His advice to present and future Alabama players: "Keep that hunger and keep fighting for something because there's still more championships out there to win. There's no limit to what this program and what these guys can do."

Lester had 48 total tackles and four interceptions during the 2012 season for the Crimson Tide.

ALABAMA CRIMSON TIDE

JEREMY SHELLEY #5

Jeremy Shelley (5) follows through on one of his five extra-point kicks against Michigan, as A.J. McCarron (10) holds, in the season-opening Cowboys Classic in Arlington, Texas.

It was the field-goal attempt of a lifetime, a pressure-packed 23-yarder from the right hash mark.

It was Alabama vs. LSU for the 2011 BCS National Championship, right in the Tigers' backyard, the Mercedes-Benz Superdome.

With LSU fans screaming and wishful Tide fans hoping for the best, the snap from Carson Tinker was perfect. A.J. McCarron's hold was quick and seamless.

In a split second, Jeremy Shelley — all 5 feet, 10 inches and 165 pounds of him — booted the pigskin through the uprights.

The field goal, as it turned out, was the game-winner. With five minutes to go. In the first quarter.

Even if Shelley hadn't kicked four more field goals to set a BCS bowl record, his first one would have been enough to defeat top-ranked LSU. His five treys, plus Trent Richardson's 34-yard touchdown gallop late in the game, accounted for all the scoring in Alabama's 21-0 whitewashing of the Tigers.

For Shelley, it was a game of redemption, not only for him, but for friend and fellow placekicker Cade Foster. Collectively, the pair had missed four field goals in the Tide's 9-6 overtime loss to LSU earlier in the season.

"The kicker is the hero or the goat," said Shelley. "And we went from goat to hero pretty quick."

Welcome to the life of a kicker.

During his Alabama tenure, Shelley was much more the hero than the goat. His four-year career — three as a starter — was exemplary. His 304 career kicking points (172 of 175 extra points and 44 of 55 field goals) is good for fifth in Tide football history. In his 2012 senior season, Shelley was the only kicker in the country to make all his field goals (11) and extra points (69, an Alabama season record).

Shelley, a native of Raleigh, North Carolina, shunned small-college soccer and placekicking offers to walk on at Alabama in 2009. Backing up All-American Leigh Tiffin during the Tide's national championship run, Shelley saw action in one game, making his only extra-point attempt and missing a 43-yard field goal against Chattanooga. In 2010 — an uncharacteristically down year for the Tide — Shelley played in all 13 games, was 50 of 51 on extra-point attempts, and 12 for 16 on field-goal attempts.

As a junior (2011) and senior (2012), Shelley being a part of back-to-back national titles with Alabama was a dream come true.

"For us to win three national championships in four years was unprecedented," said Shelley. "It means a lot, especially with all the big-time players and teams that have come through here for so long."

Despite Shelley's spot as one of the best placekickers in Tide history, his career at Alabama will forever be defined by his rags-to-riches story in the two games with LSU in the 2011 season. In the "Game of the Century" loss, after Foster's two first-quarter misses, Shelley had a 49-yard attempt blocked and made a 34-yarder. Foster went on to hit a 46-yarder in the third quarter, then missed a long 52-yard attempt in the overtime period.

Although Tide head coach Nick Saban made it clear after the game that the offense's struggles contributed to the errant field goals, the four misses in six attempts by Foster and Shelley are what people remembered the most.

"Cade and I were obviously upset after the LSU game," said Shelley. "We felt it was the end of the season for the team. And, on top of that, I wanted to be there for Cade and everything he was going through.

"But, Coach Saban never got down on us. He was always there to help us and encourage us. That really meant a lot."

Thanks to a couple of upsets of highly ranked teams, the Tide found its way back to the BCS Championship Game for a rematch with LSU. Throughout the 43-day layoff, Shelley and Foster had plenty of time to reflect on the first LSU game in Tuscaloosa.

"The week leading up to the game, all Cade and I heard from the media was, 'Will you feel more pressure in this game?' or 'Are you going to get your redemption?' or 'Will missing four field goals in the first game weigh on your minds in this one?' Believe me, we had thought about those missed field goals over and over."

In the Tide's 21-0 victory over the Tigers, Shelley overcame his ghosts of the past by drilling field goals of 23, 34, 41, 35 and 44 yards. Redemption had come.

"I honestly had planned on hitting five that night," said Shelley, who also had a 42-yard attempt blocked, a 41-yard miss and a rare errant extra point. "That's what I had thought during the weeks leading up to the game. After I made my first one, my second one was blocked. I was thinking, 'Well, what's going to happen now?'

"But I overcame that, hit another one, and then got my confidence back. I even ended up going outside of my designated range (of 42 yards) on the last one. I was on a roll, and Coach Saban trusted me. After the first LSU game, I was at the lowest of lows, and in the second game, the highest of highs. It was a great experience to kind of bring my name back.

"And since then, it has completely amplified my career at Alabama."

Perhaps Shelley's friend and snapper Carson Tinker said it best: "When we see J (Jeremy), we see a trey."

In the Alabama football kicking records, truer words were never spoken.

(Preceding page) Shelley converted 172 of his 175 extra-point kicks in his Alabama career, including all 69 in 2012. (Right) Shelley was busy in the BCS title game against Notre Dame, making six PATs in the 42-14 rout of the Irish.

When Damion Square left his home state of Texas to sign with Alabama in 2008, he was heading to a program that was not at the elite playing level it had once been — and not close to the level of other teams that recruited him.

"When I got to campus, we kept hearing that they (Alabama) had won 12 national championships," said Square. "But in my mind, I'm thinking that the last one was in 1992. That's a long time. They had so much pride about that title game in 1992. But I'm thinking, 'we've got to get something new around here.'"

To that extent, Alabama teams had compiled a mediocre 33-30 record in the five years preceding 2008, and no BCS bowl appearances during that span.

Square, however, would become part of a heralded signing class that included Mark Ingram, Julio Jones, Mark Barron, Barrett Jones, Dont'a Hightower, Marcell Dareus, Courtney Upshaw, Terrence Cody, Robert Lester, Michael Williams and Carson Tinker, among others.

What followed was nothing short of college football history. Square and his teammates — in a five-year span — won a national-record 61 games, along with three BCS National Championships and two SEC titles.

"We came here with high expectations," said Square, a 6-foot-3, 285-pound defensive end and fifth-year senior on the 2012 team. "All those guys were here to get it done at the University of Alabama — to win championships. We believed it wholeheartedly as a group. We worked that way. We practiced that way. We disciplined each other that way.

"To get what you desire, to get what you work for, is awesome," Square continued. "Being a part of a class that accomplished so much means a lot. I know these guys will win more championships. I have no doubt. But to be among the guys that began this process — that's something special."

Damion Square (92) stares down the Notre Dame offense during the BCS National Championship Game in South Florida.

Redshirted his first season, and injured for most of his second, Square started 33 games during his Alabama career, including six in 2010, all 13 in 2011 and all 14 in 2012.

He leaves Alabama a far stronger program than he found it.

"He could have gone anywhere and he chose Alabama," Crimson Tide defensive coordinator Kirby Smart told reporters three days before Alabama met Notre Dame in the 2013 BCS National Championship Game. "He came when the program wasn't as good, and that's a great commitment."

Square finished his Alabama career with 93 tackles, including 18.5 for loss, and 7.5 sacks. But statistics don't tell the full story of a veteran player who had a major role on a defense that ranked No. 1 nationally in each of Square's final two seasons — in addition to back-to-back BCS titles.

Although Square had the physical size required of a defensive lineman, he also had "special talents to be able to run around like a skill player," Smart said.

But talent alone was only part of it. Coach Nick Saban's program included such intense preparation and attention to detail that, to a man, Alabama's departing seniors said games were not nearly as tough as the week leading up to them.

"I haven't played in a game on Saturdays that was harder than the Tuesday and Wednesday at the University of Alabama," said Square. "Saturdays were the best days. I played Saturdays with no fear. I had no doubt in my mind that I was as prepared as I could be. We had the best game plan on the field with the coaches that we had in the box and on the sideline, and the best players in the country on my side. I had no doubt we were mentally stronger than our opponent, no matter how good they were."

Married to wife Brandi Square, and father to a young son, Micah, Damion Square graduated with a degree in consumer science in May 2012, before his final season. He said he couldn't have had a better college experience than the one he had at Alabama.

It also couldn't have ended on a higher note, as Alabama's 42-14 rout of Notre Dame for the BCS title brought everything full circle for Square. Notre Dame was among the many teams that actively recruited him. He had visited the Notre Dame campus back during that time.

"Notre Dame is a great university," he said, with time to reflect back two months after the game against the Fighting Irish. "The things on their campus and the tradition that they have. Their team (in 2012) reminds me of the team I played on in 2008 at Alabama. We ran into Florida, and they (Notre Dame) ran into us. I feel like those guys will have a great future at Notre Dame."

Square's own future most likely includes the NFL. But, as he said weeks earlier, as his team prepared to play Notre Dame, his five years at UA prepared him for life, not just games.

"For me, just the development all around as a player, as a father, as a son, as a man, coming here to the university, they expect you to do things a certain way, and they hold you accountable for that at all times," he said. "And that's kind of how I live my life now."

"I haven't played in a game on Saturdays that was harder than the Tuesday and Wednesday at the University of Alabama."

— Damion Square

Square made life difficult for opposing offenses in 2012 as he posted 33 tac and nine quarterback hurries for the

CARSON TINKER #51

I n a setting made in football heaven, on a beautiful South Florida night, in a game between two giants of college football history, Carson Tinker knew what was coming.

As the Alabama long snapper and his co-specialists were warming up before the Tide's BCS title clash with Notre Dame, Tinker began exchanging customary pregame pleasantries with some of the Notre Dame specialists. What transpired during those few minutes of casual chitchat spoke volumes about the two programs, where each had been, and where each was headed.

And, as it turned out, the outcome of that night's game.

"Their specialists were in awe," said Tinker. "Certainly not of me, but of our team. I could tell it right away — they were in awe of Alabama.

"They were thinking, like, 'Whoa, we're playing Alabama.' They'd come up to me and say, like, 'Hey, man, good luck to you,' and 'Congratulations on going to the Senior Bowl' and stuff like that.

"I had never heard that from anybody we were about to play. It was just different."

Call it a sign, a premonition, perhaps even a prediction — Alabama was about to destroy Notre Dame.

"We'd been there before," said Tinker, "and Notre Dame hadn't."

Carson Tinker (51) races downfield during the BCS National Championship Game against Notre Dame.

Indeed, Alabama had "been there" — in the BCS National Championship Game — three out of the past four seasons. Playing a vital role in those three seasons was Tinker, the senior long snapper from Murfreesboro, Tennessee.

Entering the Tide program in 2008 as an invited walk-on, Tinker redshirted during Alabama's 10-2 season. During the Tide's march to the 2009 national championship, he saw action in one game as a backup to senior snapper Brian Selman.

In 40 starts over the 2010, 2011 and 2012 seasons, Tinker was rock-solid as Alabama's long snapper. In snapping opportunities (long snaps on punts and short snaps on field goals and extra points), he was successful on 390 of 394 attempts.

Counting his freshman redshirt season, his Tide teams won 61 games, two SEC championships and three BCS titles. Despite the hardware, though, Tinker cites the relationships as what he'll remember the most.

"Winning all those games was great, but I don't go around thinking that all the time," said Tinker, who played in the postseason Raycom Football All-Star Classic as well as the storied Senior Bowl. "What meant the most to a lot of the guys were the relationships that we had while we were here and the teamwork and the brotherhood. Records are made to be broken, but you can't take away the camaraderie that we had."

Tinker keeps his eyes on his blocking assignment after a punt during the 2012 Florida Atlantic game in Tuscaloosa.

Tinker credits head coach Nick Saban with creating the environment necessary to achieve such lofty accomplishments.

"Coach Saban brought in great players," said Tinker, "and we couldn't have won without great players. What speaks the most about him is that he did it with great players, and then he brought in more great players and did it again. And, he did that three or four different times.

"You can look back to 2008 when Mark Ingram was a freshman running back. Then it was Trent Richardson, then Eddie Lacy, then T.J. Yeldon and whoever will be after T.J. That's just one example of the 'Process' that coach talks about.

"At the end of the day, when you ask me what my favorite thing about football was, it was the person I became while I was at Alabama. I experienced things like discipline, teamwork, perseverance, and facing adversity and fighting through it."

If anyone knows about facing adversity and fighting through it, it's Tinker.

On April 27, 2011, between his sophomore and junior seasons, an EF-4 tornado roared through Tuscaloosa, cutting a mile-wide, seven-mile-long path through the city. In Tuscaloosa alone, the massive twister killed 53 people — including six University of Alabama students — injured 1,200 others, and damaged or destroyed more than 5,300 homes and 350 businesses.

Among those students killed in the storm was Tinker's girlfriend, Ashley Harrison. Tinker suffered a broken wrist, a concussion and a severe ankle injury. After a tough summer of rehabilitation, Tinker was back on the field for the Tide's 2011 season opener against Kent State.

"Before that game, Coach Saban talked about returning to some sense of normalcy," said Tinker. "He used that game to encourage and inspire people to help rebuild our community."

The tornado became the driving force behind Alabama capturing the 2011 national championship. Tinker's ordeal and the team's response in helping Tuscaloosa's recovery would later earn them the Disney Spirit Award, presented during the 2011 Home Depot College Football Awards in Orlando.

"A lot of people hear my story and look at me and look at everything and expect me to have the 'poor mes' … but I don't," Tinker said during the ESPN-televised show.

"I have a positive attitude. And every day is a blessing. It's a gift from God, and I really try to take advantage of every day that I have."

Through his adversity, Tinker learned some valuable lessons that'll stay with him for life.

"I came away from that year with an incredible life lesson," said Tinker, who was awarded a full scholarship before his senior season. "You are not defined by your circumstances or adversity. You are defined by how you respond to them.

"I don't want to be defined by the tornado. I want to be defined by how I responded to the challenges. You can live in circumstance or you can live in vision.

"I chose to live in vision."

Tinker reaches out to try to bring down Texas A&M punt returner Dustin Harris (22). Tinker was successful on 390 of 394 snaps during his Alabama career.

ALABAMA CRIMSON TIDE

CHANCE WARMACK #65

n the wacky world of college football recruiting, where fans ooh and ah over the elite five-star athletes destined for superstar status, never should those little ol' three-star guys be underestimated.

Case in point? Alabama's Chance Warmack.

Three-year starter for 40 games. Unanimous first-team All-American guard. Owner of three BCS National Championship rings. Crimson Tide team captain, as selected by his teammates.

Not too shabby for a quietly recruited young man from Atlanta's Westlake High School, a football factory from which — up until the 2013 NFL Draft — eight players had gone on to the pros.

With Warmack, make it nine.

"Alabama was the first team to offer me a scholarship," said Warmack. "I felt like they believed in me as a football player.

"Coach Saban left quite an impression on me, both as a coach and as a person. I felt like he wanted to make me a better person first, then a better football player. That stuck with me. That's the main reason I came to Alabama."

An early enrollee in January 2009, Warmack assumed a leadership role on and off the field. Joined by a stellar signing class, it didn't take long for Warmack to realize he was surrounded by greatness.

"It was an honor to be around such a group of guys that strived to be successful," said Warmack. "Everybody in my class came in with different goals and aspirations for themselves.

"For me personally, I was just thankful to be a part of the program. My mother and I actually sat down and wrote down realistic dreams that I could achieve year after year. The first year, I just wanted to get some playing time. By my second year, I wanted to be a starter.

"For the other guys in my class, all coming from different aspects of life, they had dreams of their own, too," Warmack continued. "We went back and forth talking about what each of us wanted to accomplish. Then I started seeing how hard they were working, and they saw how hard I was working. I learned from them, and they learned from me.

"Before you knew it, all our individual dreams turned out to be group dreams. We all began working for the same goals. And those goals reflected how we played on the field. We didn't want to lose. And sure enough, with just a few exceptions, that's just how it turned out.

"Just to be a part of a group of guys that had so much desire to be successful was an honor and a privilege."

The group to which Warmack refers did quite well. From 2009-12, their 49 wins set a SEC record and tied Nebraska's national mark from 1994-97.

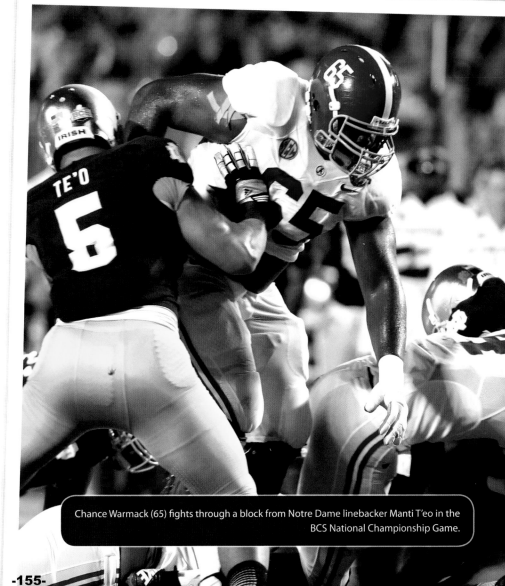

Chance Warmack (65) fights through a block from Notre Dame linebacker Manti T'eo in the BCS National Championship Game.

During the Tide's 14-0 run in 2009, Warmack saw action in five games playing behind All-American guard Michael Johnson. As a sophomore in 2010, he started all 13 games at left guard, opening holes for eventual Heisman Trophy winner Mark Ingram and All-American Trent Richardson.

"We knew that after the 2009 title, repeating it in 2010 wasn't going to be easy," said Warmack. "We had all the pieces to do it, but not everyone was on the same page. And when that's the case, it's impossible to achieve what you've set out to do."

Warmack and his Alabama teammates used their disappointing 10-3 record in 2010 as motivation for the 2011 season. A year later, in their quest for a repeat, they again used the 2010 season as motivation, but in a different way.

Warmack scans the opposing defensive line during a home game in Tuscaloosa as running back T.J. Yeldon (4) waits for the snap. Warmack and the rest of the offensive line opened holes for a pair of 1,000-yard rushers, Yeldon and Eddie Lacy, in 2012.

"We wanted to avoid what happened the season after winning the title in 2009," said Warmack. "It's hard to believe, but our disappointing season in 2010 may have been what spurred us on to win national championships in 2011 and 2012."

Warmack cites his senior season games against LSU, Georgia and Notre Dame among his most memorable. The LSU and Georgia games featured classic comebacks that will be forever entrenched in Tide football lore.

"The LSU game was very emotional for the offense," said Warmack of the Tide's thrilling five-play, 72-yard, 49-second drive to secure the 21-17 victory. "We had adversity in that one. Not many people thought we could come back and win. But 11 guys in the huddle knew we had the opportunity to be successful, and we pulled it off."

In the SEC Championship Game, against his home-state Bulldogs in his hometown of Atlanta, Warmack and his fellow offensive linemen Cyrus Kouandjio, Barrett Jones, Anthony Steen and D.J. Fluker — considered by many to be the greatest offensive line in Alabama history — overpowered Georgia for 512 yards, including 350 rushing yards.

"That game could've gone either way," said Warmack. "Everybody played their hearts out. It just came down to a few plays at the end and fortunately we made them."

To Warmack, Alabama's dominating victory over Notre Dame in the BCS title game was more about making history than the game itself.

"We kept telling ourselves we could be special and remembered for a long time," said Warmack. "To win back-to-back titles was unprecedented in the BCS era. That's all we talked about for weeks leading up to the game."

Warmack credits numerous coaches and staff members for helping him during his Alabama career, especially Saban; Joe Pendry, his line coach in 2009 and 2010; Jeff Stoutland, line coach his junior and senior seasons; and strength and conditioning coach Scott Cochran.

"Coach Saban instilled discipline in us, not just in football, but for life," said Warmack. "You can't make it out of this program without following or buying into what he's instilling into everybody.

"Coach Pendry taught me the ins and outs of football and the techniques I needed. Coach Stoutland continued teaching me those same things.

"Coach Cochran is my man," Warmack continued. "He taught me so much, not so much about football, but how to be mentally strong and crisper. All those 110s he made us run was torture then, but look what it did for us."

Beyond what promises to be a stellar NFL career, Warmack has his sights set on a food career. Yes, a food career.

"I love to taste different foods and talk about them," said Warmack. "So, I hope I can get a job as a food critic on the Food Network. A food critic. Yes, that's what I want to do."

"Coach Saban instilled discipline in us, not just in football, but for life. You can't make it out of this program without following or buying into what he's instilling into everybody."

— Chance Warmack

JESSE WILLIAMS #54

Across the rich crimson and white landscape of University of Alabama football, played by more than 2,000 men over 120 seasons, there have no doubt been many unique and one-of-a-kind players, or, as they are called, "characters."

Count nose guard Jesse Williams as one of them, for many reasons.

First, there's his size and strength. He's 6-foot-4, 320 pounds and looks as if he was chiseled out of Mount Rushmore. His weightlifting exploits while at Alabama earned legendary status. During his final summer workout before his senior season, he bench-pressed 600 pounds, causing a social media meltdown. If there's a weight room equivalent of basketball's "gym rat," he's it.

"It was nothing," said Williams, who insists he could have reached 635 to 640 pounds if allowed. "Six hundred was my goal for the year. It was good to get it on the last day of workouts and have it on film and with everyone around me."

Second, there's his hair, or lack of it. When Williams arrived in Tuscaloosa in January 2011, he sported a mohawk, causing second glances and gasps among the innocent passersby. In a "spur of the moment sort of thing," during the week prior to the 2012 Alabama-Mississippi State game, Williams shaved it off, thinking for some reason he wouldn't stand out so much in public.

"I just wanted to mix it up," said Williams. "I was running out of ideas, so I decided to cut it."

Third, there are more than three-dozen tattoos, seemingly covering every inch of his body. Calling them "constant reminders of where I come from," they are without a doubt Williams' signature trait.

Jesse Williams (54) fights off a block by a Notre Dame offensive lineman as he tries to track down Irish quarterback Everett Golson (5) in the BCS title game.

On his right hand, one tattoo reads, "I stopped checking for the monster under the bed when I realized the monster was me." Another is a poem written by his father just before he began his college football career. On the right side of his head is inked, "Fear is a liar." The tattoos, emblazoned on his olive skin, make his appearance even more imposing.

Fourth, there's his Australian roots and enchanting accent. Born on Thursday Island and raised in Brisbane, Williams is believed to have been the first indigenous Australian to earn a college football scholarship in the United States, first at Arizona Western College in Yuma, then at Alabama. There's just something mesmerizing and intriguing about anyone from Down Under, but put on a Crimson Tide football uniform on him, and he becomes somewhat of a cult figure among the Tide faithful.

"Yes, it was tough for some people to understand my Australian accent," said Williams, "so I tried to dull it down as much as I could. But it was harder for me to pick up the Southern slang than it was for people to pick up my accent. I guess it worked out well in the end."

Add together all these ingredients — size, strength, appearance and heritage — along with a bubbly and charming personality, and you get a rare, diamond-in-the-rough character so set apart in Alabama football history that his legend will be remembered for decades to come.

"Rugby taught me how to tackle, and basketball taught me the footwork I needed."

— Jesse Williams

And, to boot, Williams can claim something quite rare for any college football player — back-to-back national championships.

"It hasn't really sunk in yet," said Williams, nicknamed "Tha Monsta." "It's been an amazing time, to be at Alabama for two years and to win two national championships, the first time in the BCS era.

"It was huge, not just for us, but for the whole school and the community. It'd be tough to forget the last couple of years around here. First the tornado (in April 2011), then dealing with the death of (offensive lineman) Aaron Douglas that summer. It was a time when we as a team bonded both off and on the field."

Williams never donned the football pads until he was 15 years old. Until then, rugby and basketball dominated his time. "Rugby taught me how to tackle, and basketball taught me the footwork I needed," he said. "Because I started football so late, I had to sort of pick it up on the run. I'd watch it on television and learned a little from some coaches I knew. When I got to Arizona Western, I did my best to figure it out."

Figure it out he did. During the 2009 and 2010 seasons, Williams dominated his league as a defensive lineman. By his second season, he was the top-ranked junior-college player in the country. Primarily due to Alabama's knack for putting players into the NFL, Williams chose the Tide over LSU, Oklahoma State, Southern California, Arkansas, Oregon State, Mississippi and Tennessee. Enrolling at Alabama in January 2011, he began his short, but storied, career.

Penciled in to take the spot of All-American nose guard Terrence Cody, Williams shifted to defensive end for his first season. Starting every game, he registered 24 tackles on a defense that statistically was one of the best in college football history. In the Tide's 21-0 shutout of LSU in the BCS National Championship Game, Williams — whom Alabama head coach Nick Saban called "probably our most underrated defensive player" — played a major role in limiting LSU to 92 yards of total offense, including just 39 yards on the ground.

In the Tide's repeat title performance in 2012 — minus All-American defensive stars Dont'a Hightower, Courtney Upshaw, Dre Kirkpatrick and Mark Barron — Williams started at nose guard in 12 of 13 games, missing one game due to injury. Playing a challenging position designed to take on blockers so the linebackers can make tackles, he made 36 stops, had one sack, two pass deflections, four quarterback hurries and a blocked field goal. And, much to the delight of the fans, he was the lead blocker in many of Alabama's short-yardage situations.

In the Tide's two late comeback victories over LSU and Georgia in 2012, Williams played pivotal roles. Against the Bulldogs, after a third-quarter knee injury he was back on the field for the back-and-forth final quarter. In the LSU game, two key defensive stops — a failed fourth-and-1 attempt and a missed field goal — enabled the Alabama offense to get the ball back and work its magic in the thrilling 21-17 victory.

"The LSU game was one I'll definitely remember for a long time," said Williams. "In the fourth quarter, when the game was on the line, we held them twice. It was a tough, fierce game. Those memories of our sideline reaction will be with me forever."

Regarding the Tide's romp over top-ranked Notre Dame in the BCS title game, Williams credited the media with getting his team ready for its 15th national championship.

"All we heard from the media was Notre Dame this, Notre Dame that," said Williams. "They really built Notre Dame up. How we played showed how ready we were and how we reacted to those challenges. We play Alabama football, no matter who we're playing against. It just happened to be Notre Dame that night."

Williams credits Saban for Alabama's historical run.

"It really is a process," said Williams. "The way he runs it — taking everything step-by-step, the way the coaches handle us on and off the field, the training, the discipline, the intensity, the commitment, all these pushed us to be the best. We never really competed against anyone except ourselves."

Williams, who after the Notre Dame game received congratulations from Australian Prime Minister Julia Gillard via Skype, still has one decision to make before starting his NFL career. Following the 2011 National Championship, he added "CHAMPS" to his tattoo artwork, using the famous Alabama script "A". Now, he's deciding how to commemorate the Tide's 2012 title.

"I may put the crystal ball on there," Williams said.

If, that is, he can find a spot.

Williams had 37 tackles, four quarterback hurries and a blocked kick during the 2012 season.

MICHAEL WILLIAMS #89

It was the biggest stage in college football, and Michael Williams, Alabama's veteran tight end, was more than ready for prime time. Known more for his abilities as a blocker than a receiver, Williams played with one important credo, as he would later say: "Whatever they needed out there, I did it."

This January night, in front of more than 80,000 people in South Florida's Sun Life Stadium and a television audience of nearly 30 million, what was needed of Williams was a touchdown. He delivered, as usual.

As the clock neared six minutes in the first quarter in the Tide's BCS National Championship Game against Notre Dame, Williams slipped free in the back of the end zone and caught a 3-yard touchdown pass from quarterback A.J. McCarron. An extra point gave Alabama a 14-0 lead en route to a 42-14 rout of the Fighting Irish.

Less than three weeks later, Williams also caught a 20-yard touchdown pass in the Senior Bowl in Mobile, as if to underscore that the big 6-foot-6, 269-pound tight end from Reform, Alabama, knew a thing or two about getting into the end zone. Yet it was the touchdown against Notre Dame, on college football's greatest night, that he will cherish most.

"For it to be my last game at Alabama, a school I always loved growing up just 30 minutes down the road … I'd say that was most gratifying," said Williams.

Williams finished the 2012 season with 24 receptions for 183 yards and four touchdowns. Though not big offensive numbers, Williams' contributions played a key role in the Crimson Tide's offensive success.

"My role wasn't to run down the field and catch 20- or 30-yard passes," he said. "I got first downs, I got touchdowns, whatever Coach Saban asked me to do, that's what I did."

A fifth-year senior, Williams was originally recruited as a defensive end. That changed during his redshirt season in 2008 as the team prepared to play Utah in the Sugar Bowl.

"It was kind of funny," said Williams. "I'm going out for my scout team duties, and tight end coach Bobby Williams comes up to me and said, 'Mike, catch this ball.' And I catch the ball. And then he says, 'Now run this way and catch the ball.' And I run that way and catch the ball. He says 'OK' and doesn't say anything else. And I'm like, 'What's the point of that?' So then we go through to the end of practice. And when I come back the next day, there's a white jersey in my locker. And from then on, I was playing tight end."

Michael Williams (89) catches a 3-yard touchdown pass from A.J. McCarron in the first quarter of the 2013 BCS National Championship Game against Notre Dame.

Williams' performance improved each year, culminating in a standout final season. But despite the victories, Williams said his biggest regret was a catch he didn't make in the Tide's 2011 regular-season game against LSU. A reception would have given Alabama the ball at the goal line, and possibly a victory. But LSU's Eric Reid wrestled the ball from Williams as both players hit the ground for an interception that stopped an Alabama scoring threat. LSU went on to win 9-6-in overtime, but Alabama later routed the Tigers 21-0 in a BCS title game rematch.

"My biggest regret was just not squeezing (the ball) a little harder," said Williams. "All I've got to do is try to get a tie-up, and then they would have given it to me."

But Williams isn't complaining. After all, he leaves UA with three national championship rings.

"I don't think anybody comes to college thinking they'll win three national championships," he said. "We came in with the attitude that we were going to compete every day. Stuff just started rolling. We were fortunate to get one my freshman year. We just saw what it took, and after that it was going out there and taking care of the business part of it."

Like other seniors, Williams said it was the Crimson Tide's preparation that set them apart from their competition.

"Once a game comes, you feel like you already know what your opponent is going to do before they do it," he said. "The game is easy for us, we feel like. Practice is 10 times harder than the game."

Williams remembers when it all began, on his first conditioning workout as an Alabama player. Having played at a smaller 2A high school, Williams said he wasn't ready for the sudden change in the level of conditioning that he faced at Alabama.

"The first day, I passed out," he said with a laugh. "Coach (Scott) Cochran picked me up and he looked at me, and he was like, 'Repeat after me: I'm gonna be great. I'm gonna be great. I'm gonna be great.'"

Nearly five years later, following Williams' last game for the Crimson Tide, Cochran brought it full circle.

"As soon as the clock hit 0:00 in Miami, Coach Cochran looked at me, and said, 'What did I tell you?'

"I said 'Wow.'"

(Preceding page) Williams makes one of his three catches for 18 yards in the BCS title game. He had 24 catches for 183 yards and four touchdowns in 2012.

Alabama Is A Special Place

The University of Alabama is special, plain and simple. There isn't another place in the world like it.

People often ask me what Alabama football's secret to success is, and every time I give them the same answer. Alabama isn't special because of our highly rated recruiting classes, our coach's salary, our 34,000-square-foot weight room, our 101,821-seat stadium, or even our 15 national championships. What makes our university special is the people. Certainly, the impressive assets listed above make a large contribution to the success of our program, but all these would be useless without the people. People like our head coach, Nick Saban.

I will never forget the first time Coach Saban told me about the "standard" that we play to at Alabama. Every other coach had in some way begged me to come to his respective school, but Coach Saban simply invited me to be a part of something special and to play with and against the best. It was then that he explained that from our athletic director and head coach all the way down to our fifth-string tailback, everyone in our organization must be totally committed to the standards of our organization.

Coach explained that I would no longer be training and playing to beat my opponent, but I'd now be working to achieve the standards of our organization. He told me that achieving these standards would come only through an extremely high level of attention to detail, where every member of the team was committed to doing all of the little things right.

I would not fully understand the gravity of this commitment until my first summer workout in a scorching Bryant-Denny Stadium. After collapsing on the sideline after running 36 110-yard sprints and pushing my body beyond the limits of what my mind thought was capable, I understood exactly what striving for perfection meant.

(Above) Barrett Jones speaks at the 55th National Football Foundation Annual Awards Dinner in New York City on Dec. 4, 2012, after accepting the NFF's William V. Campbell Trophy, recognizing an individual as the absolute best in the country for his combined academic success, football performance and exemplary community leadership.

It was at this exact moment I first realized this place was different; that other people did not do things the way that we did; that other schools did not have coaches that demanded the perfection of the little things from their players like ours; that their coaches did not force each player to leap over the precipice of their self-imposed bodily limitations only to arrive at a place they never thought they could go.

At that moment, I knew without a doubt that Coach Saban was creating something special at the University of Alabama. I had a belief that, together, we could all achieve something very special that people would remember for a long time.

In turn, Coach Saban sets the tone for our program, from top to bottom. He creates a culture that demands players and coaches not only buy in to the principles of the organization, but to also hold others accountable to these standards.

This is why I love Alabama. Not only because it has made me a better football player, but because its people have made me a better man. And one day, their investments in me as a person will most assuredly make me a better husband, father and co-worker.

I just hope someday I can return the favor.

— *Barrett Jones*

ABOUT THE AUTHORS

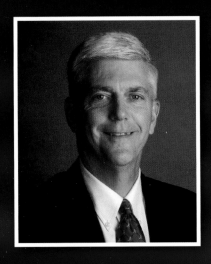

As assistant athletic director for the University of Alabama Athletics Department, Tommy Ford oversees the A-Club Alumni Association and the Red Elephant clubs.

Ford, a native of Gadsden, Alabama, earned his B.S. in Finance from the University of Alabama in 1978 and his M.A. in Higher Education Administration from the University of Alabama in 1998.

As a student at Alabama from 1974-78, Ford served in the SGA Senate, Jasons and Kappa Alpha fraternity, and during his senior year was sports editor of *The Crimson White*. After graduating from the Capstone, Ford returned to Gadsden before coming back to the university in 1982.

From 1982-87, Ford worked for the National Alumni Association in alumni chapter development and fundraising. In 1987, he was hired as assistant ticket manager in the Athletics Department, and then was promoted to ticket manager, for which he served from 1987-93. For 13 years from 1993-2006, Ford was director of TIDE PRIDE, the Athletics Department's football and basketball ticket priority program.

Ford is the author or co-author of five books: *Alabama's Family Tides, The University of Alabama All-Access Football Vault®*, the *Alabama-Auburn Rivalry Football Vault®*, *Bear Bryant on Leadership* and *Tornado to National Title #14*.

Ford is married to the former Robin Rich of Gadsden, and the couple has one son, 15-year-old John Michael.

As associate director of the University of Alabama's Office of Student Media, Mark Mayfield serves as editorial adviser to student publications on campus. He is also an adjunct journalism professor in UA's College of Communication and Information Sciences.

A veteran of the newspaper and magazine industry, Mayfield spent 10 years as a reporter and editor at *USA Today* before accepting a job as editor-in-chief of *Art & Antiques* magazine in New York City. He later served as the chief editor at three other major consumer magazines, including *Southern Accents, Traditional Home* and *House Beautiful*.

Mayfield is a 1978 graduate of the University of Alabama, where he became editor-in-chief of the campus paper, *The Crimson White*, his senior year, when he was also named the top male graduate in journalism by the University's College of Communication and Information Sciences. A year earlier, he served as sports editor of *The Crimson White*.

Mayfield was named UA's top journalism alumnus in 1990.

He is the author of *The Spaceflight Vault: A History of NASA's Manned Missions*, published by Whitman Publishing in 2010, and co-authored *Southern Style*, published by Bulfinch in 1998.

He is married to Monica Mayfield and has four children: Matthew, Stephanie, Madison and Alexa.

ACKNOWLEDGMENTS

This book simply would not have been possible without major contributions from many people, beginning with Kent Gidley, director of photography for the University of Alabama Athletics Department.

The great majority of photos we included are the expert work of Kent and his assistants: Amelia J. Brackin, Jeri A. Gulsby, Lyndsey Pugh, Danielle Flaherty and John Michael Simpson.

As the authors, we also want to express our thanks to the players and coaches at the University of Alabama for showing us what excellence looks like on a football field. We are indebted, in particular, to the seniors who took time to interview with us for this book. What they accomplished — three national titles in four years — is remarkable. And we can only hope we have done them justice by telling their stories here.

Separately, each of us has other people to thank.

Thanks from Tommy Ford:

To my friend and co-author Mark Mayfield, with whom I served on *The Crimson White* staff some 35 years ago. It was great to work with Mark again.

To Mary Hicks for her quick and exemplary transcripts of many of our senior player interviews.

To Jeff Purinton and Josh Maxson in the UA Athletics Communications Office for their assistance.

To Finus Gaston, Alabama's senior associate athletic director and chief financial officer, for his making possible this project with Whitman Publishing.

To Eli Gold and Barrett Jones for writing the foreword and afterword, respectively. Their insights on the season — from two very different perspectives — were invaluable.

To my wife, Robin, and son, John Michael, for their love and encouragement.

Thanks from Mark Mayfield:

To Tommy Ford, for asking me to join him in writing this book about the Crimson Tide's extraordinary run of success. Tommy and I have been friends since our college days, and it is a privilege to share this project with him.

To my wife, Monica, and my four children — Matthew, Stephanie, Madison and Alexa — for their love and support. They are my inspiration.

To my mom and dad, Dewey and Phyllis Mayfield, who remain the heroes in my life. No one ever had better parents.

To Paul Wright, director of UA's Office of Student Media, for his support and encouragement as Tommy and I put together this book.

To the students at *The Crimson White*, the campus daily newspaper, for their outstanding work, and for teaching me as much as I've tried to teach them.

To Gregory Enns, editor and publisher of *Crimson Magazine*, for providing me an outstanding platform to regularly cover the Crimson Tide.